Poetry Aotearoa Yearbook

Poetry Aotearoa Yearbook

2024

Edited by Tracey Slaughter

MASSEY UNIVERSITY PRESS

Contents

EDITORIAL

11 Tracey Slaughter

FEATURED POET: CARIN SMEATON

18 For Arapera and Marino

20 Aunties talk Pukekohe

21 Lael and Grace

22 The Alchemist vs Posie Parker

23 Renata anō

25 The Fate of a Thousand Spiders

26 Ariel

27 Matariki Rising

28 a musical is only 10% of the revolution

29 Dark Passenger

31 Flying whales on earth

32 He calls her a bitch again

34 My Sami Ghost

36 Te Kāhu Pōkere

37 Daughtr of the 90s

38 Morning Symposium

39 a dreadful day

41 Ureia by the Bridge

42 Beth yr a magic realist

43 Meghan Markle's Sister

45 the good auntie

46 An interview with Carin Smeaton

NEW POEMS

52	Abigail Marshall	michelangeloed / how to be art in an automobile incident
53	Adrienne Jansen	Five am among the pine trees
54	Aimee-Jane Anderson-O'Connor	Gorse
55	alana hooton	friday night takeaways
57	Alex Nolan	Working Māmā
58	Alice Hooton	AUNT
59	Amanda Joshua	Complaints re: click and collect
61	Amaris Janel Henderson	Pistol Lullabies
62	Amber Abbott	This isn't Hell, but I can see it from here
65	Amber Sadgrove	The Janes
67	Anna Jackson-Scott	To return to the body
69	Anuja Mitra	Reprise
70	Anushka Dissanayake	just a teen
72	Ben Jardine	Questions for the Self at the End of Et Al.
74	Brent Cantwell	a dredging ship
75	Brent Kininmont	Bits of Food in My Father's Lungs
76	Britt Clark	Monstrous
78	Bronte Heron	Sonnet
79	Charles Ross	Hikaroroa
82	Chris Stewart	Mary regrets her pregnancy
83	Chrys Anthemum	the duality of Jane Doe
85	Cindy Botha	penumbra
86	Cindy Zeiher	Vers(e)
87	Clare Riddell	lover's eye
88	Dadon Rowell	Firsts
89	David Čiurlionis	Waking up
90	David Simes	when you dumped me, why did you quote the hot priest from *Fleabag*?
91	Devon Webb	NEW WORLD
93	Eliana Gray	On the plane up to Tāmaki Makaurau, feeling alive

95	Elizabeth Morton	In sum
96	Elliot McKenzie	Small heights
97	Erik Kennedy	This Usually Represents a Desire to Achieve Greatness in your Social and Professional Life
98	essa may ranapiri	love as a verb
99	Ethan Christensen	my boy (so gentle
101	Evie Howell	The shape of one
103	Frances Libeau	bach 114
104	Francesca Leader	Hey, ███████, You Piece of Shit, Are You Emotionally Available Yet?
106	Freya Norris	I love you 16cm deep
107	Geoff Sawers	Too early in the spring
108	Grace Lawrence	when the pawn hits the conflicts he thinks like a king . . .
109	Heidi North	Fill in the blank
110	Holly H. Bercusson	no fat saints
111	Iain Britton	Deep down the air is rarely sweet
115	Idoya Munn	I'm writing a poem tonight
116	Imé Corkery	something to be certain about
117	Iona Winter	Lodestone
119	Jack Ross	My mother's rose bushes
121	James Norcliffe	Fade to Black
122	Jan FitzGerald	unWelcome swallows
123	Jan Kemp	Chimera — a song cycle
125	Jan Napier	I Start to tell You
126	Jane Simpson	Imagined scar
127	Janet Newman	Nocturne
128	Janet Wainscott	'In loving memory'
129	Janis Freegard	Samhain
131	Jenny Powell	*from* The Relevance of Berthe Hoola van Nooten
133	Jessica Le Bas	Driving through the night
135	Jessica Thornley	Mahuika Takes the Underground

137	Jessie Burnette	sets
139	Joel LeBlanc	Corpse Fauna
140	John Geraets	. . . from RIVERSPELL31
141	John Tuke	One of those days poetic
142	Keirryn Hintz	Eleanor
145	Keith Nunes	Mother as poet
146	Kerrin P. Sharpe	I wake @ 2am and know
147	Layal Moore	La Sylphide
148	Liam Hinton	a love poem
153	Liz Breslin	In Kathmandu, Te Tihi-o-Maru
155	Loretta Riach	Pastoral Leakages
156	Lucy Miles	Good Weather for Ducks
157	Margaret Moores	Likeness
160	Mark Prisco	worm theory
164	Medb Charleton	Wairēinga/Bridal Veil Falls
165	Megan Kitching	In the Midnight Zone
166	Michael Giacon	The kiss of light
168	Michael Steven	Strains: Northern Lights
169	Nathaniel Calhoun	blue penguins
170	Naveena Menon	if this text chain finds you, send something back:
172	Nicholas Wright	The Firebox
173	Nicola Andrews	Now that Dr Ropata is in Guatemala
174	Nigel Skjellerup	a kind of agony
175	Olivia Macassey	Millstone
176	Owen Bullock	Possibles
178	Paula Harris	If you have ever had a delayed flight . . .
180	Penelope Scarborough	Graveyard Lover
182	Philip Armstrong	Anastomosis
184	Rachael Elliott	Mild
187	Riemke Ensing	This is not goodbye
188	Sara Al-Bahar	road kill
190	Sarah-Kate Simons	Angel Parking
191	Shaun Stockley	Autumn (onset)

192 Shivani Agrawal   [in-flight meal]
193 Sophia Wilson   Do not step here, Othello
195 Sophie Rae-Jordan   Offering
196 Stu Bagby   Red Hands Cave
197 Tunmise Adebowale   A Little Grace
199 Vaughan Rapatahana   whakarongo ki ngā manu / listen to the birds
200 Victor Billot   Lost in Space
201 Wes Lee   Wearing the Night
205 Willow Noir   Obliterated Affairs
206 Wren Boyer   a crack lets in the darkness, too

ESSAYS

210 Erena Shingade   Beneath the Linden Trees: Richard von Sturmer and the Mind of Meditation
221 John Geraets   Constant Structure

REVIEWS

236 Abigail Marshall   Claire Orchard
   Hannah Mettner
242 Aimee-Jane Anderson-O'Connor   Sarah Lawrence / harold coutts / Arielle Walker
   Leah Dodd
248 Anthony Kohere   Alice Te Punga Somerville
   Jessica Hinerangi
256 Dadon Rowell   Claudia Jardine
   Sophia Wilson
261 David Simes   Jake Arthur
264 David Wrigley   James Norcliffe / C. K. Stead / David Eggleton
270 Frances Libeau   Hazel Smith
273 Jane Matthews   Ila Selwyn
   Jan FitzGerald
   Vivienne Ullrich

280 Jessica Thornley   Louise Wallace
284 Jessie Burnette   Michele Leggott
287 Marcus Hobson   Koenraad Kuiper
     Titirangi Poets
295 Mark Prisco   James Brown
     Rogelio Guedea
     Tim Upperton
304 Medb Charleton   Diana Bridge
     Elizabeth Smither
     Stephanie de Montalk
312 Michelle Rahurahu   Ruby Solly
317 Naveena Menon   Jane Arthur
     Morgan Bach
     Sudha Rao
325 Sara Al-Bahar   Khadro Mohamed

329 **CONTRIBUTORS**

343 **ABOUT POETRY AOTEAROA YEARBOOK**

Editorial

Writing from the red house

The day I wrote my first poem I was 12 and I didn't know what I'd done. I was living in a house I hated, with a man at the head, a place of hurt. That man had just kicked my sibling into the street and I was left behind in shock, and I hid and spat something onto floral stationery meant for thank-you letters to long-distance ancestors who had no idea about the hellish house on the hill where I felt so unsafe.

The poem came out bad, fast, hot, double vision, carved hard onto the page. It was something between dog bark and lullaby, between bird call and bared teeth. I must have been trying to both kick back and console myself, to rock myself and roar. I had zero models except shitty pop songs and musty old classics in a mouldy pocket-size book of rhyming poems (ironically, lifted from that man's stash, not far from where his shotgun sat loaded). It was a blurred, noisy mess, but that didn't matter: it was about wreckage, it was about choking. It was more like an exorcism than a moment of art: it was automatic, it was autonomic. It piled up images out of every disaster movie I'd seen — the sea rose up, the house turned red, all the elements blazed against it — cuts of wide-scale pain to collage over the small, dirty scene that had just happened at my door: that man's hands, my sibling knocked onto the asphalt.

There were some facts it couldn't hold fixed yet, in frame. But it held something, it *was* something, it had *done* something. Jerky manifesto mixed with fucked-up sob, prayer crossed with not-yet-suicide note. Whatever had left my body and rushed onto the page, it had something to do with survival. I had no muscle in that ugly house, no armour, no comeback, no voice. I couldn't see a way not to stay and get broken, there was no other shelter. But I had a piece of paper that didn't say thank you, that didn't stay silent, that scraped black lines across the flowery page where I was meant to whisper the sweet nothings little girls are made of. I couldn't fight, I couldn't flee — but I could write. And those words didn't freeze, and they did not fawn.

We are so often detonated into poetry by our nerve ends. We flare to language when life trips our red wire. Whatever skills we acquire along the way — to direct the current, to regulate the blood jet — the *why* of poetry so often remains the same. We hone our craft and we learn to rein it in with the cortical, the critical — but most poets know the fuse, the force, the source is, as Colum McCann says, the 'electricity of suffering'.

It pays, of course, not to openly declare this: the market tends to like its poets shining not bleeding, waving not drowning, chasing the commercially angled spotlight, not casting the glare back onto our scars and the system that leaves them. There's a special kind of shame reserved for artists who risk wearing heart's blood all over their sleeves. In the poems that poured in for this issue, though, the evidence was everywhere: there's a breed of poet who is writing from the red house — writing for their lives, not for likes — and they are bent on taking the risk, on witnessing patterns of wounding, and taking apart the machine that put them there.

So, trigger warning: this is a book of revelations. Apocalypse lives here, and it's not going away, and these poets aren't apologising for facing it. The same flood, storm, flame that surged through my first-ever poem is now the permanent forecast. Our days, our islands, our skins, our seas, our skies wear the stigmata of late-stage capitalism, and these poets have no interest in concealing it. They are writing — McCann again — 'so as to not fall silent', because they see the ruins of silence all around us, its dead institutions, its gouged earth, its bound hands, its nullifying currency, its foul oils, its crushed species.

The point where personal emergency meets collective oppression is set alight again and again in their poems — they refuse to let the hurt be siloed, classified, diagnosed, dosed, written off. They do not cower before the structures built to quietly retraumatise us. Their work 'hits the hazard lights' and summons all its craft to 'hammer and wonder and cry . . . banging the tin of disappointment/and worthlessness bringing up the spectre of future/homelessness, and poverty and sickness and all that befalls'. They know the place to expose the workings of power lies deep within us, where it brands our tissue, twists our responses, sells our safety. This is the nexus that the system is so vastly invested in us *not* seeing, the flashpoint that poetry is so inextricably wired to force out into unforgiving radical light. '*[H]ow would yous rate the pain?*' asks the opening piece, and the answer resounds: '*sistine*'.

But this comes at a cost. And reading this year's poems, I felt that weight, that toll. If the imagery of end-days was ever-present, so too was the echo of how much our poets pay to speak it. It can be a tough haul from our first poem to our last one, and after long-term exposure to the system we are so often eroded into poetry, hollowed, ground-down, exhausted into it — poem after poem that came in this year sounded voiced from 'the end of the rope', uttered 'right up against this precipice', hanging on by 'a whimper blight a slow sapping', a statement of precarity, struggling to preserve in the lines the frailest shred of hope.

There is nothing to be gained by not calling it: one prevailing theme this year was suicide. We all know we are losing poets. Not so long ago, we lost Schaeffer Lemalu. This year we lost Paula Harris. The witness of how deep those losses run — and how much we desperately need to treasure, to nurture our poetic community to guard against bearing any more — was undeniable. Connection, which is poetry's tender, is more crucial now than it has ever been.

So when I inevitably waver in writing this, and want to score it through with a backlash of triggered red lines, I hold on to a message from this volume's featured poet Carin Smeaton: 'I'm tired of living life as though we're walking on broken glass and might get cut by the peoples who are probably the ones who caused the pain anyway.' And I watch late-night footage of Sinéad O'Connor, who looks punk and wounded, and mutinous and starved, and worshipful and like she's had the shit kicked out of her, saying artists are meant to be messed-up vessels, willing to lay everything they have on the line so the system is made to see its pain, and I think of Paula, and what this world does to its protest singers.

And I read the book that another poet links to me, Anne Boyer's *Garments Against Women*, which reminds me that 'to feel deeply, or to admit to feeling deeply' is so often treated as 'inadmissible' because it has everything to do with 'money (poverty) or violence (how money and bodies meet)', and the 'pity, guilt, and contempt' it provokes are themselves 'feelings of power . . . the emotional indulgences of those with power or those who seek it'.

And I listen to a student who happens to bring into my classroom words from Audre Lorde I first heard long ago but need to rehear: 'When we are silent / we are still afraid. / So it is better to speak / remembering / we were never meant to survive.' And I tell the girl who wrote that first poem — on the days when she still feels as though she's living in a house she hates, with an unsafe man at the head, with her siblings still getting kicked into the street, a place of hurt, climate-destroying, near unsurvivable — that she has a community around her now, to write with, to strive for, to fight on beside.

And more than anything I think of how, late last year, I stood on a stage performing one of Paula's poems — because Paula, along with a host of other poets, was helping us to salvage a journal that was red-lining — and how later in that same show I played a mangled seabird trapped in a box and then an inmate telling of the prison grid that locked them into the emptiness.

And out of her poem's final words — which were 'nothing. / it means nothing. / nothing' — poured all the impossible love we struggle to protect against those perpetual dead ends.

And if this year I need to stand up and read Paula's poem when we launch this issue — which sounds the word 'run' in a storm aimed straight from her body 89 devastating times — I will. For her.

Featured Poet

Carin Smeaton

For Arapera and Marino

she talks about you
Arapera
she talks about you lots
and fucking
i wish i'd listened to her sooner
sweet mānuka
i wish i knew then wat i know now
it's only natural
it was always u
and u was all sex
yr daughter says
yr sister and keri might agree
you talked lots about it
bodies & the fireflies
& there was lots of them
glistening wet brightenings
beams of particles
uenuku coming
lots in the mornings most
long lazy hazy hotel days
naked
in hong kong
yr daughter told us all about it
(yea)
honeysuckle
she was embarrassed
but happy
in reflection
u wrote
from the kitchen
a songbird
in full voice

in all its monstrosity yr
touch yr blood, yr bone deep bites
yr lost eye tooth
drunk on cuts
straight down the sternum
& if it was (especially) memorable
carried ways further down
from inside yr womb
into yr poems
into this one even
50 years later
(or abouts)
(and much inferior)
(aroha mai <3)
by me for u
thru my bung eye

Aunties talk Pukekohe

yr calling in to sort the whenua & calm the cousins while yr at it u
travel all the ways from whangārei aunties swooping in like kahu
from a waking sky

u weaves in & out of matua's shelves just how tāne does breaking
code n kete in a tropical low u says who's this white guy & wtf does he
know?

u knew that nen we all knew her she never recoverd they really put
the boot in we remember Pukekohe with its fukd up colour bars

cinema hellscape stores porn lovin bishops pukekohe with its
headless angels grieving schools nothing 2 see here fukboys mayors
of mediocracy

pukekohe the kahu in the sky sees u as do i (the ancient trees of tāne)
we all knows what u r & we all kno wat u did   ae

we knows where u live

we was only around for yr market gardens sustenance n five spice life
but even we left after that we never went back eh whāea survival of
tha aunties

once upon a time u says we wāhine had mana and we was treatd as
such but not now eh pukekohe fuk u we only want land bk we jus
want our mokos to feel welcome

Lael and Grace

i always see them at countdown ponsonby Lael & Grace grounded
in front of the olive oil & othr fancy condiments i know Lael from
W's class who (by her own admission) is unfairly seen as tha grumpy
auntie at the tangi

Lael's young & Diné she flew here above jetstream with her
frightfully featherd wings strapped 2 her arms spiriting her all tha
ways from portland to tāmaki she follows tha sun across tha horizon
tha sun she says always forgives u

it forgives u for calling yr boss a cunt it forgives u for mistaking
seattle for portland it forgives u for losing yr shit cos portland's in
washington grace says it's easy 2 be mistaken we all are even Lael but
tha sun don't care

Lael used to work for seattle library they both love libraries Grace
says she visits central all tha time i want her to see our heavens our
livin breathin roof when the mārakai is ready when it opens up for
matariki (if i'm still there)

when it's gotten green n grown as big as gov grey's concrete cum
footprint on tha whenua auntie wanna tour too libraries change so
quick she says she visits central every year just to keep up with tha
goss she's happiest here with a coffee

The Alchemist vs Posie Parker

auntie's an Alchemist a Shapeshifter
A good lil arawa girl gifted but auee
Lucky that day she weren't at the hui
when the west wind blew into the wharenui
With their big flash shoes swayin hips in front
of our elders all them muscle mens
Yea bitch lucky auntie weren't present
she woulda ripped off dem 'lashes
thrown em out wit tha red stilettos Out
u blow bye bye bitches i mean fuk that shit
manipulating kawa twisting tikanga
biological or not Don't matter the storm
b like the kuis theyre ovr 80 barefoot n seein
hi-fem n butches our nens Own us
They own our shoes our soul our eyes n tides
so out u flyy theyr the whenua we breathe
ha! it's amaze u was ever allowd in

Renata anō

I don't know why renata stops
she slaps
she lifts an arm :o
it's so sudden it's like she'd rather do this
than shake my hand or just say hi
kanohi ki te kanohi nē
ever since lockdown
i never saw it coming
no signs no inklings
just a loud hard sting
of a crack of a whip
on denim
did u do this kinda thing in paris before lockdown
or after
renata?
renata
let down yr long hair
down to yr waist
bluu grey & silver fate
& why not kuīni
wear it like a korowai
on yr heaviest of days
(when papatūānuku is bleeding out more molecules than rain)
scent of a jasmine flowr
base of an oil
we r all just memories
we brought to the pools
that time eh renata
(til a lyin tit stole them while we was in the shower)
why not sis
fly down the escalator
(sketches by darwin spillin outta both sides)

like u won't ever get caught
behind me you'll creep
i watch my back
u watch the dew on a leaf
still the leaf calls out
Witch!
daughter of an alcoholic
sister of a seer
do u feel safe now?

The Fate of a Thousand Spiders

she's descended from generations spinning webs on the wheelie bin
surviving a lifetime of rubbish days droughts floods & plagues

he loved his job once he even picked up a couple of kids droppd them
at school in his big rubbish truck the kids loved it (but whāea walkd
them for the rest of the term)

he was always somebody's uncle somebody's waving uncle
somebody's weaving spiderman uncle ted in a big cool truck wantd to
pick up tha little ones on rainy days

but it never rained once that summer so the mayor got on his knees
beggd the mighty Waikato 4 water & surprise (for a price) he was
successful

the city could buy the sky wit its desperation but the spiders still
made their homes in it undr it between the powerlines in the streets
on bins sky lovd spidrs spidrs lovd sky

It was nobody's business but their own & uncle in his big yellow
truck taking care lifting full to empty never disturbing the web of
peace spinning round

& round she was an ancient one from generations of hairy ones a
whakapapa of scary ones beelining to the sky to hineahuone & she
was all woman uncle says yea

> lil fevers in the sky spinning spirits til we die te ara o te
> hau uncle says

Ariel

u never thought yr name was cringe
till grandad changed it to AJ
AJ he said
when we move town when u start a new school
then we'll change it back to ariel
yr new friends will be older there none the wiser
& they won't tease u about it then
(yr cousins included)

Matariki Rising

For Dad

we sing for him before he goes
me & my sister late for the funeral
our stepmother rolls her eyes
we even got us a ukulele
(we wasn't gonna sing her dum song)
we're throwing hibiscus so he don't look so lonely
throw them flowers right into the sky throw them colours
straight into the hole the wood looks so heavy
too polished too ded
i turn to princess she got style n flair
(& good hair)
so close to pirongia eh
princess says yea
the faeries might come play
we giggle n snort but the spiders stay quiet
weaving their traps down the main street
a rose-town a massacre
a church and a cock
we follow our loss
connecting a match to our sweet valley daze
my sister regrets throwing out her smokes again
40 bucks
fuk he'd laff if he was here

a musical is only 10% of the revolution

annaida's read les misérables
60% of it
that's what she says
i think she's showing off
typical angel
is she trying to scare me?
i had to read
every single line she says
as if the devil forced her
as if it's dreadful torture
fork thru tha eye
needle up tha nose
then she goes says good luck
to me touché
u might finish it off one day
tick it off yr bucket list
listen cunt i was an angel too
once i sang tha entire musical
as earth was quietly warming
underneath a kōwhai tree
in the domain with brian
we wasn't even drunk
i was ghost of voltaire
he was javier
we was just a fraction

Dark Passenger

pete's gone awol
he's been missing for years now
didn't show up for his dad's funeral
no one knows where he is
what he's doing or who he's with
whether he dead or alive
pete ha!
whadda joker
last seen in perth
surfing
under the sun
blazing as always
he told us all about his
shark fights countless
great whites in tha deep dark
blu   every xmas of course
good ol pete
all that bravado
& don't forget the meth
that too
for the triggers
a blunt for the ticks
yea pete yea u
left ya wife when she was pregnant
fuck she was a saint
last time we heard
u was missing yr kids like crazy
crying so hard
u got tha stigmata
blood for tears red as rubies
warm & sticky
it leaks out holy

we all carries it round with us bruv
trauma from the past
trauma from da present
it never really lets go
some of us tho
r jus very high functioning

Flying whales on earth

he tells friends she's loopy bitch that no one else will touch her
he thinks he's a saint for just being her husband
(but he's not even that good looking)

he takes her to westfield to shop for good times
all she sees is cum stains on a samsung dryer a harvey norman bargain
she gnaws on her thumbs til tha cuticles run red

stinging puss bleeding he calls it disgusting yr crazy he spills
& threatens to leave her divorce in the imax
(but that's never stopped him from sticking it in lol has it)

she's dreaming she's riding four fine flying whales
do u see them she asks him lifting her face stretching her spine
he berates her as usual whales don't fly she points to the sky babe

before they swam they flew thru tha blu stars of life is not life on earth
she calls for her whales her children her babies to gather together
she's ready she says to return

He calls her a bitch again

he mutters under his breath she barely hears him but she kno wat he's saying she's not dum eh auntie he turns up every day at her desk it pisses her off big time when she works the big work counting the stats

he's just a hōhā nuisance she's getting so far behind she might never catch up she dreams those dreams where she's running as fast as she can going nowhere getting nowhere never reaching her destination the beautiful blue roses she treads on won't never pick themselves up

fix your hair she tells herself go for a tiny tidy ponytail tucking stray strands behind the ears then bloody well just get on with it she's bad ass eh auntie she be sure to sanitise cos he's near his mask falling under his nose like an afternoon nap it might simply fall right off right there and then a fleeting shadow of a shrug floating effervescent to the floor a lonely apparition there to settle for the day

he never bothers to pick it up it's the same as always he expects her to but she jus gives it a long hard stare cold as ice she'd rather pick up a bloodied tampon just the thought of it make her sanitise which make her knuckles chafe everyone knows nobody likes no sign of the period do they

sanitise sanitise

use the one that smells like gin

till yr skin peels off & yr flesh turns thin

(cheapskates they always get the cheap stuff)

did u kno he wears the glasses held together with scotch tape he squints at the world thru fractured lil cracks magic multiples it's a wonder he can see anything at all but he always sees her lord why couldn't he use his own wifi she got more important things to do workin the lord's work if she didn't do it quick it'd be money down the gurgler just another job lost it's written all over her face

priorities

most peoples get it but not him with his scotch taped glasses &
runaway mask sitting himself down telling her another da vinci code
theory more painful than when they was wedded that time at st
benedicts he wantd to b more closer 2 jesus than her

Fanatic

moon time will always be our beginning
end & empty in between

she sighs loud when auntie flo visits she tries hard to prepare but it
never helps she shouldn't even be here but here she is trying to get
shit done bleeding bloody mary she sure she gonna pass out in her
own sacred river

how'd he like it if she stole his pride?

how'd he like 2 b haemorrhaging between the thighs?

bet he'd lose it big time

go kaka

eh auntie

he called her a bitch again

bitch eating crackers

say cheese she says (she picks up the scissor)

say cheese she says (she'll go for his liver)

My Sami Ghost

Mike stood up for justice & the sami
at the scandinavian library seminar

before he was found dead in his
small mt eden flat last year before

anyone even knew he had diabetes
at the service Pete talked about him

with a tired yet full n loving heart
autumn at saint matthew-in-the-city

where Mike became a jesus ghost
a rainbow an ally of tru

sami-spirit sittin nice spiced unquiet
embalmd looking back at his life

tappin n thinkin & thinkin n tappin
on tha boss's gold stud ear

u never knew me did u mizz?
U only knew me wen i was ded

(but that's ok)

embers from the candle
candle in the wind

u never cried a single tear u just wants to cum in
to wear your favourite red hot lipstick

& flash yr corporate buzzwords
sounds too sweet like hospital jelly

cold as ice cream condescending
my sami ghost licks off flat tones

off yr lips & off yr bones
babe so thin they'll never nourish u

they'll never kiss the morning dew
or raise the dead in April

Te Kāhu Pōkere

guo pei sewed a hawk at the tip of my tongue
& i waited for her to open my words
pierce a taste-bud
prick a feeling with its fierce hook
her black wings stretching out wider
than a mile never missing a bite
we never did what we was told
we never smiled for a soul
(that wd merely burn embers into our humiliation)
at the office i kept my dum mouth shut
for 2 days no more
i could only hold the hawk for so long
picking out stitches with a wide-eyed needle
til she circled the sea with motorway rage
she flew past ōkahu where sewage lurkd
she flew over sweatshops where we used to work
can u see the director at the window now
polishing off her staff like illegal pāua?
that bitch wd eat her own children if she could
stuffing her belly full of a million salty clauses
nothing will ever satisfy her
nothing never does this gaping hole
in the tāmaki isthmus where te kāhu flies
where either the sky will take us soon
or the cranes will

Daughtr of the 90s

when she gets promoted to usherette
a baby blu eel carries her all the way up
to mothership she's hovering high

she lets the underaged in to see keanu reeves
she lets the only lonely flowers
of the world in for free

she lets the district angels of the court sleep
all day in the back row
(cos that's what keanu wd do)

mākutu can keep her bottle of O negative
let her watch let her touch herself
let her talk herself up

let her go curse tha lawyers in the gold class seats
they're groping her ass in the dark again
& they still havnt paid for their high thigh massage

lyf's all lux in row K

bk at the arcade the kids all dress up to winona
she's making a comeback
they got all that big suit retro shit

lovelorn daughtrs of the 90s
recharge the sad gurls at the skyy arcade!
nothing will ever stop them

Morning Symposium

she tastes like kava & she knows it
at the morning symposium wasted on 6 cups
pretty potent bigger than tits
big buckets big a drenched papatūānuku
shakes her head at the sheer scale
her son would flatten the city if he knew
jealous n hōhā taking her so-called infidelity
out on the world
even after a nice cuppa tea
dear
after all this time & you've never calmed down
the morning was much quieter full of light
snacks she drank too much in that circle
travelled around the pacific she moves
in her world with her new (much younger) lover
who smells like earth just like her but saltier
with a hint of dashi zest a splash of moon n moana
taking her deeply digging into wet folds
with his out of date iphone
such gentle probes shadow licks
flames of fading ghosts line the beach
he shows her the masks
taller than houses
(more powerful than jesus)
he says the missionaries hated them
took them to god knows where
nobody knows anymore
can u hear the waves?
      can u see the ocean?
they own us

a dreadful day

i regret wearing my old
pink butterfly belt
too close to the groin for u my lover
of lavender lady of leisure scorpio rising
up from the ground floor
witch
i don't wanna get on yr bad side renata
get slapped with a migraine an earful
of lazarus like cum from a high priest
i get it i do/ i'm a dreadful disgrace
not dressed the best
like it's not as if we live in the Ukraine is it?
Working the day shift
in a hospital ruin
we're jus here in our temple
taking notes for security
for the good of the peoples
on the sacred floor
we watch the james rain
the youth on her roof
wave
it's always a close call
they already know the drill (like
they catch our pulse even at this distance)
diligence
we note colour width of wings
level of boredom kicks risks falls
& menstruations
the faves of the day the laffs thru the smear
U might say it's a fetish but hell
we care renata tells us often enuf
bout these sweet lil emergencies

incidences
only on lorne street
only in summer only in this heat
one minute torrential the next it's just
auē the disgrace
it drives us all
over the edge

Ureia by the Bridge

I tried to hang myself under the harbour bridge
(wouldn't that be the one not too far from here?)
they just keep coming atcha I hear the nurse say
like we r the pulse of all her problems (but she jus need some sleep)

hauraki is the hub of distraught and sweet comebacks
& such a comeback is surely tonight
the bridge will make sure of it
lighting the world up like a recharged dragon

& there's nowhere to hide so enter the taniwha
she says hold my hand spark to skin knife to vitals
cutting the waves wit the fin split n cut of an orca
skimming the surface in a revelatory moment

reflecting raspberry orange or whatever tf u ordered
wit an umbrella on top showing the place
where yr soul wants to sit under the night
at mermaids bar drinking up the light n shadow of hine-nui-te-pō

wen she's not dancing she's cussing up a storm
nurse says she'll let it slide 4 now
bargaining with the waitematā is ongoing work for frontline staff
and sister we hear u we're tired yr tired

we don't expect nothin much (4 our sins) cos we're already
pretty much (u kno) rootd but look at us!
blinking battling breathing out of our gowns
the bridge's never lit up like this before

Beth yr a magic realist

beth couldn't really get into
one hundred years of solitude
she just didn't have tha time
how she tried between work & study
& looking after her wee ones
now love in the time of cholera
now that was easier!
tru that's what
alexandria thought too
those of us who forget passwords
always remember the story
it flies high in tha sky
tha homesickness
tha yearning
the kite that flew to london
titiri at the water clay
red ochre on his hands
āe chief
mwah! shine on pāua eyes
feather of the aute they say
fly faster when u lengthen tha cord

Meghan Markle's Sister

u never wantd to go
to australia
leave cat-pig behind
with friends
bk to the river
away from the sun
the sky on their tongue
caught in yr throat
burning bye into
yr ancestral wings
let them go hun
they'd never make it
thru customs anyways
crammed into yr suitcase
like a whakapapa happy meal
kiss me goodbye too
go live with mum
under the circling planes
louder than dragon flies
they won't be around for long
them open spaces
will lick em up clean
show u how to sketch
trips in & out of yr hometown
away from the weddings the wendys
the house flipping bullshit
paint yr forever home
in melting shades
of lunar
the mexico trips
thru the desert
(& the pink

deep crevices of the old man's face)
will be the best thing
to ever happen

the good auntie

when auntie was the tooth fairy
she'd call her lil angels from faraway (australia)
sis im skint but im trying i'll fly over soon
2 bubs over the moon so pretty so funny
they'd offer her all the pearls in a gappy smile
& she'd purr like a lactating kitty
deep in her bones she vibes if tha mauri
gone noho find yr happy place
if yr wairua's broke go home how bout it
for a nice hot bath? a deep slow fuck?
a cheeky lil visit to the 3 dollar shop?
(what u mean e hoa it's 5 dollar now)

An interview with Carin Smeaton

Lives strung between powerlines and wheelie bins, hellscape Westfields and emergency wards: the speakers in Carin Smeaton's poems 'touch yr blood' and take oppression apart with 'a fierce hook'. Their stories track through urban spaces that resonate with capitalist hurt, hard-edged voices holding 'spark to skin knife to vitals'. Her razor-cut lines deliver sharp critique of 'the bankrs in the gold seats', throwing a world of trickle-down privation into stark relief, as characters up to their necks in minimum-wage life talk baseline truths, a chorus of the blunt and wasted, gutted and resilient. In brutal conversation with 'trauma from da present', with an unflinching take on its colonial roots, Smeaton's poetry lights up the ecosystems of the city, zooming in on those who live in its chokehold.

TS: I don't think anyone could read your work and not be reminded that the voice is a muscle, a thing of motion and action, of sinew and force. It's one of the things I've found so gripping about your writing since I first encountered it — how voice in your work takes us 'straight down the sternum' of your speakers into the energy of character, right into the heat and beat and gritted teeth of raw full-frontal speech. It comes across as a bone-deep directness in talk, no frills, hard-edged, that has everything to say about your characters' lives. How much did this voice just rise from your gut and how much have you had to work to get it on the page?

E te whānau, tēnā koutou katoa.

Nei te mihi, nei te aroha <3 Ko Kurahaupō te waka, ko Tararua te maunga, ko Muaūpoko rātou ko Safune, ko Hūrai ōku iwi, ko Tāmaki Makaurau tōku tūrangawaewae, ko Kazma rāua ko Yuga ōku tamariki, ko Carin Smeaton taku ingoa. Tēnā koutou, tēnā tātou katoa.

Kia ora Trace, thanks for featuring my mahi in *Poetry Aotearoa Yearbook 2024*. I feel really honoured because you have always been one of my favourite writers and editors. The damaged, brave voices in your narratives really inspired me to write more from the fire in my belly. In spirit, if you were a singer-songwriter you could be Sinéad O'Connor — and true, I totally agree with you about the gut — that our voice comes from some kind of sub-layer of the soul, memory (via the sternum!) and the land. It's a relief to be able to use (exorcise) this demon (trauma) in my creative work. Good therapy!

TS: Cityscapes — in all their concrete shine, their gridlock neon — seem core to your poetry, too; your characters feel grown from an urban ground-zero that's packed with industrial gullies, jammed with dead-end jobs, studded with motorway stars. How much of your poetry is inseparable from Tāmaki Makaurau, as your tūrangawaewae, your turf?

I don't think I could write outside Tāmaki Makaurau. Come to think of it, I don't think I ever have! Maybe I need to get out of Auckland to see! Auckland's a hostile city actually. I mean, I don't know any cyclist who's not been hit by a bus or an SUV. You got to be pretty stubborn and resourceful to kick around in this town. Bus stops in the city can be pretty dodge. Post-lockdown Auckland feels the edge even more perhaps. I try to walk everywhere no matter the weather (rain or plague). Auckland's got the most amazing rainbows. I don't get cat-called anymore, so that's nice. Like other Aucklanders who walk, I suppose I get the time to sense the spiritual and ethereal in places. And the beauty.

TS: Speaking to lives that have dropped through the system's cracks, been dealt shit hands, the missed out and messed up — 'pretty much (u kno) rootd but look at us!' — also feels like a key drive in your writing. How urgent did it feel to you to use your poetry to light up the frontline reality of lives on the brink? How much impact do you hope/believe the act of writing poetry can have on these circumstances?

I don't think poetry is transformative — not exclusively. It can be cathartic. Poetry might have some (transformational) impact on us if somehow it's a source of sustenance and connection. For me, writing poetry is a meaningful way to connect with people whose stories we're privileged to listen to and learn from. This year at a wānanga with Waimarie, we were discussing the devastations from cyclone Gabrielle. If the land was taken from under our feet, would we have a stable identity and collective memory to rebuild with? Sharing memories, stories of the land and peoples and connecting through poetry, mārakai or whatever brings people together kanohi kitea — whanaungatanga can help us be more resilient collectively as a community, especially in times of dispossession (nothing new).

TS: Your work bears hard-hitting witness, too, to an Aotearoa with 'gov grey's concrete cum footprint on tha whenua', tracking a colonising force that has 'really put the boot in' to the land and its people. Was calling out this damage and fighting its ongoing cost always a focus in your writing?

I think I've always written dispossession into my work; I mean, that's how I feel anyway. *Tales of the Waihorotiu* acknowledges the natural world interwoven into cracks of cityscape. I love so much how there's history, knowledge and whakapapa (like from Robert Sullivan and Hone Tuwhare) carved into the ātea of Queen Street acknowledging the taniwha Horotiu. No amount of Guv Grey could sanitise the history out of te taiao our natural environment. The land under Toi Tāmaki and Central City Library was gifted by mana whenua Ngāti Whātua Ōrākei to Hobson so Auckland could be built, and it is vital for the city to acknowledge and reciprocate mana whenua and this act of incredible generosity in its everyday values and spaces.

TS: The presence of 'the aunties' — as straight-talking, warm-hearted, no-bullshit champions of cultural resilience ('who's this white guy & wtf does he know?') — feels like a real lifeline in your work too, with so much gorgeous, larger-than-life badassery attached to these unfailing wāhine toa. Did you set out to pay tribute to them with your poems, or did they just muscle their way in, 'calling in to sort the whenua & calm the cousins while [theyr] at it'?

A beautiful thing my workmate Mel and I did in 2022–23 was working with whānau. We showcased toikupu from mana wāhine and tūpuna who were published in earlier editions of *Te Ao Mārama* anthology. We were really inspired and awed. These rangatira were, and still are, fierce advocates for justice. Their works are totally unsanitised accounts of socio-cultural history and their experiences as wāhine Māori living in Aotearoa New Zealand under an imperial Western system. Saana Waitai Murray's whānau, Ngāti Kurī, continues Saana's legacy of rangatiratanga that she grew from Wai 262. Her poem 'My Decree' is insanely brilliant. A must-read!

TS: '[O]nce upon a time . . . we wāhine had mana and we was treatd as such but not now eh', declares one of the 'aunties' in your poems . . . I'm curious whether there are wāhine writing now who are a source of inspiration, or whose activism galvanises you?

I deeply admire kaupapa Māori groups and whānau who guide the mahi — groundbreaking transformative projects through values like kaitiakitanga, aroha, whanaungatanga and manaakitanga for our aspirations and wellbeing. Lots are kick-ass poets, too — Vernice Wineera, Bub Bridger, Arapera Hineira Kaa Blank, Evelyn Patuawa-Nathan, Teresia Teaiwa, Trixie Te Arama Menzies, Georgina Stewart, Ngahuia Te Awekotuku, Roma Potiki, Linda Tuhiwai Smith, Marewa Glover . . . mana wāhine! They walk the talk! They're brilliant, staunch and wick funny! Please check out their poetry and other vital works.

Recently, outside Aotearoa, Mariana Enríquez has inspired me to write more terror because I love how she uses this genre for social and political comment.

Ngā mihi nui ki a koe e te rangatira for giving me the opportunity to answer these excellent and challenging pātai. It's been a real honour to write this lil collection for you alongside the illuminous mahi of many more poets in our kete. Thank you for having me. Aroha nui xx

New Poems

michelangeloed / how to be art in an automobile incident

& the impact, well / the damage wakes up to itself / ticks & freezes / clock hands crack back / window writer / radio stutter on the trip & drop / dense, raw cheeks on shatter / on sleet / on barley sugar glass

catch the air in tooth sockets / split enamel on tar grit / burst salt from the swell of chewing gum tongues

then hook on the sharp flood / stuff papers into overfull cupboards / fleshy fingertips bloom back till / bulk folds under & in / those pins / threaded into thumbs / a *Giovanni* notebook slips from the seat / concertinas on the dashboard / red lines slurry through the windscreen / ripple to blue / *how would yous rate the pain* / *sistine* / a bludgeoned laugh / temple bruise / unbuckling / bone bent up under a chapel ceiling / mixing purple paint / below skin

Adrienne Jansen

Five am among the pine trees

The moon, surprisingly, is still
hanging between branches.

The last owner walked through these trees
dragging the damp air into his damaged lungs.
He picked up brittle bits of kindling
that he stacked in piles in the woodshed.

They were still there
when we bought the house
from his widow,

because no matter how much he believed
in the enduring warmth of open fires,
the bright flare as twigs caught alight,
pine logs crackling along splintered edges,
his lungs had other ideas.

I can hear him now,
his shoes shuffling through the needles,
the pause as he breathes the struggling air,
his fingers scraping out a bone-thin stick
and I pick it up and lay it on
the stack in the fork of my arm.

Gorse

After Gregory Kan's This Paper Boat

We climb the farmer's stile
clamber through wet clay
slip down the mossbanks
We drop into the stream and stand with our hands out
Fantails
chatter and swoop
skim our fingertips
We call out to you
ask you to haunt us here
skeleton leaves floating in the flurry
widowmakers wedged in the branches
lurid lit gorse
lupins the same bright purple you often wore
We spot a kingfisher high
on an old telephone post
follow the trail upstream
sidestep cattle pugging and
tractor tracks
like rockpools filled with saltwater and pain
bloodworms squirming red.

friday night takeaways

she is sick so we are sad

grey; the primary colour palette to your face
i colour inside the lines

stains of curry and sticky rice
orange plush running round the plate
most of it sticks to his face

friday is an outtake, slow and private
it isn't the real thing
he forgets his cue to hold my hand
i tell him again that it's fine
i pretend not to know the meaning
the bloopers, the missed lines

the conversation holds itself
two women in front of me
never able to admit defeat
two hearts of Michael Hill gold, matching bracelets
i am reminded, sickness

chemotherapy and goodwill wishes
all it took was stage 4 breast cancer
to get flowers once a week
like christmas every day
your hair is blow-dried and brave

i wonder if i'm nicer to you, special treatment
that i don't mean to be giving,
or is it merely a chorus to chemo?

i space out, stare at the table
think about your life
how many hearts are strained
by your dwindling days
i know you don't know me well
but i wish you weren't sick
your skin matches beige cardigans
the days of spray tans are gone
the future looks paler than this
white laundry sheet, sock amnesty
a thing i won't say, a thing you can't fix

i forfeit a thought
drag myself to the present, when she laughs at what we say
she is sick so we are sad
but we are happy today
— friday night takeaways

Working Māmā

I can't possibly watch another episode of *Paw Patrol*.
But I drop you at daycare
and keep the soundtrack on in the car.
Don't cry before work. Your makeup looks good.

On my desk:
pile of papers
coffee cup *(every hour you wake me before 7 is one more sugary
instant)*
a Hot Wheels car you slipped in my bag.
Your love note.

I present the car back to you at pick-up.
Like a diamond ring, it reflects in your eye.
You've forgotten the morning
when you tugged at my skirt
pressed your face to the window as I drove away.

We drive to the beach.
You throw stones
poke a jellyfish
say 'whoa' about a stick.
Early evening sun throws a sharp splash of yellow on to an unmoving
ocean.
Bays curl and dip in the distance.
The whole city weaves tracks over the water from us.
People pay two million dollars for a doer-upper
with this view.
You never look up at the ocean.
It doesn't matter when you have a new stick in one hand.
You never look back to the morning.
It doesn't matter when Māmā is here now, her hand in your other.

AUNT

stepped out of her gumboots folded her best red party dress. Waded
naked out to sea. Come back, come back, we shout. Between waves
watched her head bob up past Arkle's Reef Boogie board down sand
dunes along the creek bank we cut Toi Toi spears. Sun Leopards
leap as we crash through bush. Across the wooden bridge old Mr
Rapata shouts bugger off Chocolate cake, lemon squash Gulls shriek
fight over crusts of our egg sandwich. Among rock pools tiny pink
sea anemone suck our fingers wrinkly. It's cold it's getting dark tide
rushes in tumbles the walls of Jane's Princess Castle. Jane cries won't
put on her Jandals. Says Aunt promised to come back bring her the
purple spotted egg of a man hating Komodo Dragon and a baby Llama
Jack finds a red backed crab under a scoria rock

Complaints re: click and collect

You want us to start using click and collect
But there's something I love about supermarkets
You worry for the time wasted
searching for the aisle with the laundry detergent
Wouldn't online shopping just be so much more efficient?
But I like the well-lit aisles, I like the people
consulting dear hand-scrawled lists, checking off text requests
for late night chocolate from dear ones
Dear one, in India neighbours walk into my grandmother's house
  unannounced
You want to know: *Why? Isn't that a security risk?*
Because they have gossip, because they know there will be chai
and apples and a cool place to sit
because they know the door is open for them
If you happened to get sick in that neighbourhood
you would wake to find the fridge buckling
under the weight of pepper chicken, lemon rice and hard-boiled eggs
Community looks different in a big city
But in supermarkets people are still bound together
by this one essential rite:
making sure to feed their bodies, sustain
each other
We are all going home
to cook, microwave, snack
I hope the kids trying to hoodwink their mom
into buying fruit rollups
manage to pull it off
I hope the man in the suit debating by the ice cream section
decides to keep the good carton in his trolley after all
And you; lime scooter lover, reformed motorbike owner
the shopping cart is your steed in these aisles, *do you*
remember when you nearly crashed into the old man debating

between rump steak and chuck?
He was kind about it, said we seemed a sweet young couple
You tell that story whenever
our friends come over, your sister, my dad;
Does click and collect come with
dinner time anecdotes?? Anyway
I don't know very much; I am very small
and it is my very first time being alive
But I do know that people need to be around people
Can we take some of these ice blocks home?
We could walk them over to Catherine next door
I think her boys would like them

Pistol Lullabies

Pulling braids

Walking reins

The thinnest angel wings
not free to wonder
in a fistful of hope
harnessed by

                      smoke

Her teardrops float

the CRACKLING of a chest
Pistol lullabies
taking shots at a moon of flesh

A panting deer
in hunter's hole

               gazing

                         gazing

                                              cold

This isn't Hell, but I can see it from here

You left me a folded paper crane. Packed up with the rest of your things, light blue construction paper sandwiched between books and photo frames.

I don't try to decipher what it could mean. The chemo had left you slow and waterlogged in a way that even now I don't think I could fully understand. You moved slowly and spoke to people that only you could see.

It wasn't until months later that your dad found the crane and posted it to me, slightly squished in a brown envelope.

I'm guessing it was meant for you, he writes. *It says your name.* Along the top of the left wing, I am printed clumsily in handwriting that looks nothing like yours.

It must have hurt, I think. That is the part that I keep coming back to.

Near the end, even breathing took effort. The blue paper beak is neat and crisp, the point of the tail is sharp.

It must have hurt, forcing your fingertips to fold and turn and press. Again, grief makes itself known in its cruellest form. The last memento that I have of you is a portrait of your pain.

You handed me a pocket Bible that we tore the pages out of to roll blunts with, and I said *This is the worst thing we've ever done. Are we going to Hell?* It was one of those nights where the air was warm and you could fall in love with anything.

You laughed and said nothing. Actually, you said:

This is far from the worst thing we've done. You flicked ashes onto the grass. *Besides, God is a busy man.* I'm sure he gave up on us years ago.

It was summer, humid and sticky, and I kept wishing that I had met you earlier.

The pages of the Bible were the size of my palm, and I couldn't stop laughing nervously, as if we'd be struck down where we stood.

You weren't religious, and neither was I.

It is not until a few years later that I start praying to a God I do not believe in.

In my dreams, I give you everything, all at once.

I give you my blood. My teeth. My tongue.

I give you a folded paper crane.

I ask what it means.

I give you a bandage. A tattoo. A pocket Bible. I press my hands together and pray until my palms are sore.

I give you a switchblade. My open palms. A breath.

I give you the sun.

I give you my hands, but the movement tilts us both off balance and we stumble into the lake. I am so scared that we will sink beneath the surface where no sound can reach us, and I won't be able to find you again.

When I wake, I am still searching for you, before it is too late.

Maybe it is.

But I sit outside in summer, when the air is warm and sticky, and a folded paper crane still holds your fingertips.

It's crazy how long love can hold its breath.

Amber Sadgrove

The Janes

if pregnant call jane

a shadow
underground angel resistance
from the testosterone pumped air
clamped lips for the mars men
masked up
strapped down
two dimensional play thing

if pregnant call jane

he calls them the red squad
she is our saviour
forced motherhood hidden in ink
release
blood orange pressure
a metal dig

a
silent
fuck
you

if pregnant call jane

a solemn drive from
the place
hidden gravel
the pigs blinded cock
exposed

to
the front
musty hands
shaken sheets
hidden in white picket fences

if pregnant call jane

the unmarried venus
she must walk down lucifers lane
keep the equilibrium
for her own safety

if pregnant call jane

Anna Jackson-Scott

To return to the body

It's common, for me, to exit
    the body

I keep seeing you — a flash
    in shop windows,
        a hint of a face on a bike, someone striding
        like you   down a street
bright, in daylight.

How have I forgotten? this is not
    that city, you don't live
            here,

        we're an entire continent
                    apart.

But there's history, here, and not all of it's
    wanted.

The first time I left my
    body, I scrubbed my skin
    down
    so many
    layers,
revealing pink
    mess
    beneath.

    When I think
of it now, I still can't see
how a minute point of focus can obscure

an entire   whole

I'm obviously missing
        something . . .

Am I more or less
a body if, to think
        now,
it doesn't much connect
        to the same
                person?

Soft return.
Next line.

What to write
        next?

Soft return
Soft return.

Reprise

what a shame we can never replay
a season: pull it back and start afresh
with a clean sheet of dawn.

the fog — call it winter's
parting gift — makes hazy islands
of our mountains and monuments,

breathes over the boxy roofs
of our predictable houses,
on whose fences stand tūī

unbothered by our complaints
like feathered sentinels
awaiting a more urgent assignment.

they're brash in a way
I have to admire: like the bumblebee's
bargain with gravity,

the heavy engine of her body
pedalling the air, held aloft
for beauty, against sense.

Anushka Dissanayake

just a teen

/
Tearing out grass,
laying down,
uncaring of stamped stains,
frail memories lit gold,
clouds braiding hearts and alive mothers,
so i take a chance and whisper to mine
       Mum i'm sixteen today
hope rouses cremated bones,
ravens cackle but,

Mum's still asleep.

Kicking webbed tombs,
disturbing the dead with toppled hate,
i leave
/
Pupils dilate in ecstasy,
hazy groping in
crowded rooms with drugged ambitions,
burnt fingers on rolled joints,
to fit in, throats exposed,
veins too young,
drowning in amber liquor,
stashed in duffel bags to pour down,
splayed limbs and paralysed opinions,
i am one of them,
       popular
       congrats.
/
too fat, ***too fat, too fat***
beneath ribbed cages,

swollen fingers clawing inside,
ripping fistfuls of fatty organs
emptying out,
      i convulse,
my spine melding
      one with the rim of cold porcelain,
knees numb,
crouched in mercy
      heaved dry
finally pretty
/
a teacher once told me i was bright,
that night i dismembered the running grooves
of the heavy thing inside my head,
combusted the papers marked red
100s with singed edges
into the   waste

a teacher now tells me i'm a fuck up,
finally i smile
      thank you
/
i walk the edge,
spreading wide my skinny arms,
relishing one last hit,
before flying
      that was me.

Year 11 winner of the *Poetry Aotearoa Yearbook* Student Poetry
Competition

Ben Jardine

Questions for the Self at the End of Et Al.

And I got to the end of the rope
and noticed that there wasn't much
distance from the frayed sinews and
a concrete slab just beneath my feet.

the fact is I'm dead
and my brain is too,
and I'm meeting with other dead
selves, like I am
a game show contestant
who just last week
won the million dollar prize
and this week
is on *SNL* and *Oprah*.

the fact is I have questions, like:

why does no one care about
the death of their great-grandchildren,
just the death of themselves

and

why am i so scared

of tomorrow;
of New York;
to paint my fingernails
the fervent crimson of identity;
to quit my job for the creased cover
of a dim-lit bookstore;

to devote my days to the winnowing
taste of personhood.

my self is not myself unless
i take some time from
the shuttered eyes of sleep

the fact is my eyes are
shuttered for sleep
and my self is on rotation like
a big hunk of meat in
the window of a kebab shop

the fact is my eyes are
covered in dust and grit from
kicked up Cambridge Terrace asphalt
the fact is my eyes are a
singular moon
hanging above Mt Victoria

the fact is my eyes are dying too

a dredging ship

when I was young there was a sad sound
a barely perceptible grinding on and on
a sea-and-steel-wet echo in the smog
slowly slicking ashore on a five o'clock shadow —

then the dredging ship was always there on the bay
emerging
out of the back-and-forth of a morning mist
keeping our harbour deep enough —

and now I garden near this picket line,
picket fence, hem-line sometimes
between grandchildren and the smoke of another ship
but I find even I am wanting, wanting —

so, I hedge still another bottle
— brush thicker, deeper, more ambiguous
but it's a funny sort of no, this fist of red fingers —

it's a funny sort of consent this slow erosion
but I have everything I need now,

now I'm broken in and deep enough —

Bits of Food in My Father's Lungs

The tissue across his windpipe isn't closing tight.
Your drawbridge, says the doctor, *is broken.*

At the deep end of his delirium my father nets
a response. *Clothesline*, he slurs.

A line that extends and retracts, perhaps.
Like the one in my first backyard.

It replaced the stubborn rotary line
and the need for that tongue of concrete slabs

to the middle of the grass.
I told my father I would get a jackhammer.

Just stand the slabs on their ends, he said.
Gravity will break them on a well-placed rock.

He said the only tool I had to hire was a trailer,
to cart away the pieces.

Monstrous

is the waiting in this sharp, white tooth house
it's getting dark
the small frame of my body is a fern
curling under
the weight of the
sinking sun
each darkening smells of
iron and dirt
of Ghosts

they spread inky fingers across my chest strum my
ribs as I try not to
breathe
try not to give
air to the noise
lie still. let earth spin.
reverberate internally as

heavy, clawed feet raise floorboard edges
there — a rattling breath
in: two, three, four
out: two three four
repeat until
light
until this body is not my body
until this body is not
until this body I
misjudge

time space
light comes back but
I am older and

Bruises spill black — stains on my neck — the shape of my hand
I have been crushing my throat in emulation for so long
that now grown
now woman
I rattle
different, yet still —
Monstrous too when I
breathe

Sonnet

Coat season. The trees are getting bonier. At the market
in Union Square Park, I buy a loaf of bread too big for me to finish
by myself, knowing it's what I'll do anyway, taking care
to seal the remaining slices inside the bag to prevent them
from moulding. Count many things on my list of cruelties
but never the intentional waste of bread. Even as it hardens
I refuse to throw it out, despite it being cheaper than most things
in this city. I don't tip the vendor and she smiles at me coldly.
We're all just trying to survive, I say to myself as I leave
to catch my train. In the West 4th subway, a man in rags is bent over
his hands, wrapping a dead rat in a sheet
of clear plastic. I watch as the small body disappears
inside the transparent layers. I want to be noble too
I think. Love the ones that matter least.

Hikaroroa
Inspired by Mary Oliver

If you get the right few firm friends
together talking in a kitchen
maybe there's religion in that.
I'll try to pray
by watching the geese fly overhead
from where I am
physically
on the porch with my friend
as she has her morning smoke
in the fresh air
by gazing out at Hikaroroa, remembering
that this rounded peak
six hundred and sixteen metres
high on the horizon
had its name long before the Reverend James
ever set foot on this soil.

I'll sit in the red lazy boy chair with my feet up
running my fingers over the blackened holes in the left arm rest
cigarette burns
from when my friend's nana used to chain-smoke
in this lounge
before she died
and we'll pretend this space is the confessional:
'It has been good to be here with you both'
I place my thoughts down
and wait to see how they are received.
'Then stay, move in' she says to me
'You really could, if you want' he echoes her
so I hang my keys on their spare hook as a joke
right after

but hey, what the hell,
I could get used to this.

The roundabout walk to the beach feels like a pilgrimage
with the sun lowering
casting our shadows longer and longer
and the grapes that we steal
to share along the way
and how it ends as it does
with our stock-still group
staring out at the sea
as its surface sprays up
slamming the pillars of rock
that rise up on this still-sunny side of the pā.
We make it back by evening to dance around the hazy lounge
to the dumbest songs,
and one friend says
'It's so f-cking funny how you're all going so hard to this sh-t I f-cking
love you guys'
in one breath
from where she's sitting on the couch
a glorified single mattress.

I can wake at six and wait
for the sun to rise at seven
and experience something similar
or akin to ascension
while watching the low-hanging morning sun
come through the grapevine
bright citrus slices of light
that create bold shadows on my wall
because my friend's father sold the curtains
I enjoy witnessing each day
as it approaches and recedes

watching the sun rise and the sky expand at night
stars lurking and emerging
and there, too, is religion
felt in that mundane vigil.

Year 12 winner of the *Poetry Aotearoa Yearbook* Student Poetry
Competition

Chris Stewart

Mary regrets her pregnancy

I dreamed of doctors who knew
how to help me through a water birth.

I was certain a caesarean wasn't an option.
Wise men I knew said look to the stars;

when it's cold, wear an extra layer.
My rules for life were always apologise;

always pause for red skies in the morning.
As a nurse I lived where others died.

I'd seen too many births to remain still.
In the evenings I walked along rivers

to watch ducks scurry after bread crumbs.
I spent my money on blue cotton to sew myself

a headscarf. I never revealed to anyone
the angel of my dreams said laughter

at a distance sounds like crying the way
fighting cats at midnight sound like babies.

I never told anyone. Instead I flapped
around like a dove in a barn, and

my baby walked on water before
he flew away and fell down like a stone.

the duality of Jane Doe

I find you
in the title cards
of a *silent film*
tiny white flecks
flickering on black

eyelids forced open
against ocular disturbance
so that I might absorb
your *narrative*

must I tie my fingertips
to the *couch* cushions
so they don't
reach for you?

delicately knotted ribbons
straining against my curiosity
my ache
to curvet
into your hushed *pixels*

*

breaking free
as your *story* comes to an end
I go for a walk
to calm myself

fill my days
with slow motion picnics
accompanied by the ghosts
of unidentified women

until I think I spot you again
skipping
between the **trees**
at the edge of the park

Mother **Nature**
in a bomber jacket
your roots
forever embedded
in my pores

plant parma violet kisses
on my forehead
rip my hair out
from the roots
and ask me to choose between
forest
and
screen

Cindy Botha

penumbra

'... *moonbeams communicate no sensible heat to the bodies on which they fall...*' — *W. C. Wells,* An Essay on Dew, *1838*

apogee or perigee drag the water
forth and back
tides, mud crabs and eels
menstrual rivers
melancholia
lunacy, which is the weight of moon

some things die, stranded on the sand
others drown
still others are not born

moonbeams say only *I am here*
I am still here
offering no sensible warmth
just thumbprints of leaf-light
sea-sparkle
moth and owl
grunion massing
stingray and wildebeest on the move

from the just-seen disk
of a waxing crescent, earthshine's
gauzy light

my mother's hands are full
of flowers, no perceivable warmth
what holds me
is gravitational cold
I whisper *I am here*
she is far
past hearing

Vers(e)
After Georg Büchner

It is with each quarrelling line
that any attempt to writhe a way out is
met with another way into
an abyss, where every shape of every word is
discordant, capturing its own
perilous intention
of *kissing oneself to death with one's own lips*

Never should words be genteel, even as
each line written to perfection
rises by the clock and
eases into exhilarating displeasure
only to be reluctantly cast aside from weariness

Never should there be clear conscience as
one unhaunted by bad intentions, attempts
to sleep well, live well,
and *worm out of rotten verses* . . .

Clare Riddell

lover's eye

pull your beaded necklace tighter
around my waist
let your giggle-water slop
over the side of the glass
(or down your throat)
pierce my chest with the needle
from my gramophone
draw glitter and blood

plant lavender under my windowsill
snap your suspenders
smear dirt over your brow
tip your flat cap
and promise with a wink that you'll be back tomorrow
if you are the flowers
then I am a crystal vase
ready to shatter in an   instant

the frames in the hallway may be smeared
with colour and oil but you are
a gilded lover's eye
a dagger strapped to my thigh
with a violet ribbon
the last little trinket
in a stained-glass cabinet

look but don't touch

Firsts

Her first kiss happens in a park
in the dip below the ridge that rises to the cricket
changing rooms and public toilets
it's like the side of a barrow at Stonehenge
she thinks of the chalk horse, trapped in the hill
between the Celtic fort and English Heritage giftshop

Her first kiss is in small-town New Zealand
where they say 'milk' as 'muwk' and raise their boys as sports players
her knees are scabbed from the fall when they were all running
from local girls who called them sluts

Her first kiss is watched by three friends
two girls and a boy
it's nearly second base or number seven
on Georgia Nicolson's snogging scale
— apparently being groped outdoors makes it more noteworthy

his tongue feels like a slug between her teeth
hands in too many places
she doesn't know what to do with her own
guesses this is just what boys and girls do,
straightens her elbows and fingers
keeping them flat against her sides, out of the way

Waking up

Waking up to the same knife ache
inside the bone   dry and left out all night
time seems to stop every time you   stop talking
to me. i never thought you wanted me to
be someone else   every time you tried
no one   wanted this   except them who
ever after.

It's the final   melt down   the walls
are closing their shut down
the conversation   veered away from   comfortable territory
strapped in
to the machine   breathing for us
even though there is no us anymore nonsense
and it really is over   the top

of the mountain sits
like a fucking pariah lost in the
pages of a book
maybe the bible
or something you said to me
with the express intention of
flaking out when the fantasy got funny
pages and pages of the shit
you were saying

i get it   in the neck   every night-time blankness
would you have ever asked   for the bill
if i went to the   pain point   they brought up
a young child   trying to get through
their dinner   without bringing it up
in the next argument.

when you dumped me, why did you quote the hot priest from *Fleabag*?

on that last night i thought you tasted like pennies
some signal it was the start of your period or whatever
     i didn't mind   you know i'm a feminist
but i get now you'd riddled yourself full of bullets

couldn't look at me as you
chewed away the gunpowder
     from under your nails

     I love you, but I am not in love with you

     and when i detail how we're interwoven
     in backseat fucks and ticket stubs

Chet Baker and Dolmio jars

     you tell me   *It'll pass*
     like you're the protag in this thing

     but pretty soon you'll break fourth wall
     and eyeball the barrel of that
     imaginary camera
          only to understand that no one
          else wants to watch.

Devon Webb

NEW WORLD

A chicken & mushroom pie alleviates the dissociation associated
with mid-tier threesomes spontaneously plucked from the screens
of Hinge & flavoured with the incohesive emptiness of the fourteen-
dollar cocktail I spilt at Southern Cross. A European man gives me
salami as a goodbye fuck-you thank-you present & it tastes like all the
things he wanted to say but couldn't find the space to. I do not have
the space to. The salami is still in the fridge.

I have dumplings after the first half of too-much-to-do. We made it
just in time. The moving van waits outside as I smoke weed on the
couch, I get far too lost in my own distractions sometimes I get far too
lost in my lack of home. One of the men from the moving truck is a
boy & he feels like home but the kind you've never been to or come
from & probably wouldn't go to if someone didn't take you. He says,
you must be smart if you read so many books. The books are all in
boxes, they'd be prettier if they weren't. I say, they're all fiction, I'm
emotionally intelligent, I inhale empathy. He understands in the way
of someone always learning. Our vape clouds merge in the cab of the
truck. If only smoke could hold hands. Everything's so high up here,
even if this moment on top of the world is fleeting I feel so very high.

The carpet isn't vacuumed. You know you have to change the bag,
right? All my furniture so recently abandoned sits on the debris of
somebody else's chaos. The flatmates don't have personalities . . . I
leave, if only for something to eat. That path behind Percival Street
looks even more like a Studio Ghibli movie in this weather. I've never
seen so many dandelions in one place. I've got a lot of wishes to
make. Rounding the corner onto Boulcott a man & I make meaningful
almost-eye-contact like we both turn back & we're just out of sync,
oh too many of these moments are fleeting.

Everything's got meaning though or is a metaphor for something else, 'cos outside New World I see another man, I do more than see him, as he smiles at me it feels like my life-path is altering beneath my very feet & my being is being undone & when I do it back up I know it's gonna be better than it ever was before. He looks like a watercolour painting. He looks like anime. He looks so surreal set against this backdrop of triviality. His eyes are so blue blue blue like sky going inwards like sinking so quick you rise. Nothing is tangible anymore. His name's on my tongue like an acid tab & I didn't have to wait for this trip, it was instant.

At New World, I get a rotisserie chicken but I can't eat it, my stomach's so fucking full. All the dandelions are inside it now with their wishes blowing round.

Eliana Gray

On the plane up to Tāmaki Makaurau, feeling alive

Genderless folds of the earth's body
molten on the skyline
the moon
spreads over Ōtautahi
snow melt clouds
scope out secret lakes

Everything's made up of want
when you're waiting

Rubbed against maskless strangers
we're all hopers
up here

The sandwiches will be fresh
the family outings fun and frictionless
Anything's possible
when the sun's going down
and arrival's an hour away

Make a playlist
watch the lakes turn silver
turn mercury
turn blood, orange, descent

Turn into the worst
most earnest version of yourself
hankering
to gullet the stars
but not talk
to the seat mate

Wait patiently to tell someone
  I saw Onetahua in the dark
  I saw the first star come out

In sum

I want to be the kind of person who juices the engine at night, alone.
A person who pats the dashboard, hits the hazard lights and drives
over a bank. That is me.

My nurse says, state your assumptions, and mine involve a time
when vinyl upholstery in a panel van carries me from church to
church like a lucky charm.

I want to believe in something so small it is significant,
maybe a supermassive black hole with a voice like Kenny Rogers.
My nurse says, state some personal qualities.

I want to be better like the sky is. I want to be God narrowed
to the pinch of an aerial. My transmitter barks
up into space from where the spouting rises from the rhubarb grove.

It is asking *is there anyone?* and it knows
the answer is the loneliest thing.
If I could be a person

I could be the sort of person who winds the odometer
back to the hydrothermal vent where nothing became
something so viable, a registry office emerged.

This is life. I want to be the sort of poem that carries
agony to the next guy, who whispers *is there anyone?*
like it is a joke from a festive cracker. I want to know others

who pat the dashboards, hit the hazard lights, and drive
over the banks. This is the thing. Poetry is no one
to record the tyre marks as they leave the road.

Small heights

I lost entire weeks. It seems bizarre that I have
so few memories of such a time. Although if
you think about it; we already don't remember
much of what we say or do. The brain discards
memories like used tissues. My car's nose is
nuzzled right up against the berm. I am nuzzled
right up against this precipice.

I betake myself to my mattress, fold my
t-shirts in neat little rows. Dream of different
houses, of black cattle running below my
levitating body. Tend to get so submerged in
my own despair, an exponentially multiplying
occupying force. The rain has bought the
vermiform of my guts to the mud-slicked surface.

The lawnmower has run lanes into the
waterlogged grass. A flood of weak winter
sun haloes the trees. Riotous colours coalesce
in a poisonous tumble. There is a gaping hole
encased in bright barbed wire. I tore a whole
page out, wrote down everything I knew. A
would-be paralysis judders in my axons.

The ocean stutters. The nervous signals are
jilted. The smell of gasoline in the biting air.
Ocean-born elvers bite the heels of those who
venture into their depths. There is no place here
for a heart that revolves. Standing in the grey
never-ending sea I wish I could trace its smooth
throat.

This Usually Represents a Desire to Achieve Greatness in Your Social or Professional Life

Back when I had a drug-induced psychotic breakdown and was convinced that there was a helicopter following me across the city, I didn't consider the helicopter's possible symbolism.

What can I say? It was a selfish period of my life.

I thought a searchlight was focused on me like a grievance. I thought I had petty and powerful enemies pursuing me.

But it was nothing personal. Like in a dream, the helicopter was a big force and I was a little one. Wealth flying in the air while I trudged the avenues. The promise of the future rising clear of the dust of the present. Or a firefighting helicopter ready to dump water and fire-retardant polymers on me, a quenchable fire.

I went to a bar I'd never been to and explained about the helicopter that was following me, and someone said, *Wow, man, weird. Have you done something bad?* And I said, *Yes, but nothing I thought was that bad.* And they said, *Sometimes it's hard to know how bad 'bad' is.*

love as a verb

she's out in the backyard hand-sawing the
dead plum tree into movable parts
removable from the property
no falling fruit now
the birds hunger
for premature flesh
the tree's spindly fingers go in the bin
to save us from their touch

///

she walks to the nearby creek
to gather harakeke
boxcutter in the right
karakia in the left
turns the words into air and
leans into the bush
to cut away the elder blades
so as to not destroy the heart

///

she takes the bark and dyes it
into the strands
a feather plucked from a sacred
bird to replace a shell
hanged by turmeric lengths
reshaping the metaphor and
moving it into a forest I've never been to
but want to go

Ethan Christensen

my boy (so gentle

my boy (so gentle
the vale between his top
lip and nose) leans in
close (the soft moments
we coalesce) and brushes
cupid's bow against the
ridges and dips of my

ear (throbbing hot as
red blood cells pump
across the cartilage) and
in each secret whisper
he short-circuits (like blades
of kikuyu clicking a hot
fence) my vertebrae with

pulses of electricity that
arc up my back (up to
the nerves spread across
my head like the fingers of
an open hand) and my veins
shiver like a surge of
tide on a pebble beach

and for each small breath
he draws (from gold air
thick as the sap of a felled
pine) he can shape the
sweetest phonetics (a
pop of saliva as his jaw
undulates and the tip

of his tongue touches his
teeth) while with mine
i taste dried sweat on his
collarbone (lapping up
crystal patches like licking
velvet) not entirely sure
where he starts and i begin

The shape of one

Black-red plaid
dress is overhead
subtle soft lesbian
zip on left hand side.
She is grasp around
under-boob
and lack thereof.
She is short breaths
and she lets the wind
draw back curtains
of perky underbelly.

Bra is alien.
She is black and lace
and hidden in shelves
well away from the
plastic curves displayed.
She is four hooks and
stiff pole posture.
She smothers your ribs
like a good first impression
to the in-laws.
She preaches that
silicone or foam
can close the gap
to find femininity.

Jumpsuit is stoner
and mum.
She shops sales
and hangs over
wide shoulders

like Greek god.
Pull strings tight
corset conductor
constricts the
orchestra waistline
to find shrivelled sound.

Panties are pawn.
Disposable to puppy teeth,
disposable alongside
loose flesh packaging
that overflows onto thighs.
The term boy shorts
redacted
alongside product that
fits unfortunately well.

Closet is reusable coffin
and I plan on staying here
until I am found.

Frances Libeau

bach 114

limping out
from old earth
each mooring rope
slaps with cheek

see time's noise
igneous; sore.
do you hear that clear
pitch underwater?
a wet echo
sloughing at the
crickets' keening
rub

emergent pink &
gleaming as sunset
clusters of liquid cloud
drift toward another
scene. the book
butterflied — each stitch
of spine a disc, slipping
from the next

i know your layers
flense with each frame
your earthworm scars
shivering. *to see well,*
you say, *close your eyes*

Francesca Leader

Hey, ██████, You Piece of Shit, Are You Emotionally Available Yet?

For Paula Harris

I'm not saying I blame you for everything — you didn't
birth her, raise her, or damn her
with self-destructing genes. By her words, you gave
her great pleasure, some affection, and too much hope, and
it's for that last of those things that I hate
you.

I really don't care how smart you are, how broad-minded,
how competent a lover. You're no different, at your core, from
men who slide into my DMs seconds after a post about my
divorce; men who, seeing self-harm scars on my daughter's arms,
ask for her number; men who'd accuse me of careless candor,
impugn my daughter for looking years older than fifteen; men who
think sex with crazy, sad chicks is hot, and don't give a crap
what becomes of them
after.

I'm saying all the evidence suggests that you used her — took
what you wanted, and left the rest. I'm sure you rationalised that she,
a grown woman who'd said she was down to fuck — not to be
loved — was responsible for her choices. But we both know she
couldn't have danced that last tango all by herself, without
you.

I'm imagining too-late acceptance emails — joy crumbs,
unconsumed in her inbox: *Dear Paula, We loved your work and would
be delighted to publish it in our next issue . . .* I'm thinking of being
wanted, and how badly she wanted it, and how long she crawled,
from crumb to crumb, on the trail that finally took her into the
sea.

I really don't care how many poems you inspired, ███████ —
if it hadn't been you, it would've been someone else. Because you —
you piece of shit — aren't special. But she — PAULA —
was.

I love you 16cm deep

I'm here to tell you it started in a kitchen
On crate chairs and a white picnic table
    Why didn't you help dig the grave?
    Two dozen Steinlager couldn't get an answer
    But the fresh dirt under my fingernails kept me asking
I'm here to tell you that I closed my eyes and when they opened again
I was cleaning abdomen skin with a torn grey t-shirt
I'm here to tell you that alcohol isn't a defence and blood splatter
marks
Are ricocheted onto a wall from a cheek wound
That knives used at uppercut force make clean cuts
Driving through a heart; lung 16cm deep
The seatbelt never put its hand on my shoulder
Or wrapped around my hips
And campervan drivers imagined the mess of no brakes activated
On hairpin cliffside corners at 120kms per hour

I'm here to tell you that a blood transfer on a Premacy door handle
Was the last time I held my brother's hand

Too early in the spring

One vein stood up like a skyline jackal
serotonin floats on blue meltwater
her skin was steaming, gas lamps guttering
sticky silverblue muslin but she couldn't sleep
angrily held his hand so the nails dug in, long grass hard stalks
were you made of webcode, loose paper spills
the shredded coils of seven-year-old accounts
tallies from an old woman's notebook
bound in the corduroy offcuts from her husband's coat
and he was an extra volume, she thought he'd never listened
but once she was gone he sat at the oil-cloth table
laboriously wrote out all her long-lost stories
posted them *en masse* to the parish magazine
who printed them week by week as the days grew lighter
all but the one where she'd criticised President Jackson
and by the time the apple blossom was in flood
swallows carving up the clear bright air by the bay
he'd sewed them all in sections, then bound that with boards
covered with a floral print cut from her Sunday dress
and you wonder if he'll die with that book in his hands
some Sunday evening in the orchard, wasps stumbling about
blitzed on fermented fruit he forgot to gather

when the pawn hits the conflicts
he thinks like a king . . .
After Fiona Apple

and when the highway
becomes a tunnel and i, a
cover song of my sister . . . i
didn't
even change the words only the
font slightly. it's like the
game where we take turns
hitting one another
in the backseat of the car
just hard enough to see bruise through seatbelt, but then she spits on
    me and i swear i'll
kill her. that's where our difference
lies, hers to unsettle,
mine to slaughter: for every spare school sock we fought over there is a
naked foot, and a tuna can emptied in the
other's schoolbag. we were becoming
products of a city only silenced by catastrophes, practising our own
    fires and
quakes, practising silhouette shaving,
ribbon tying,
saying phrases like *opulently corpulent,*
to
use on ourselves and each other. when we stared into the same
vanity mirror i would see
double you, my eyelashes trite with overuse. The
excess,
your red
zone after the earthquake.

Heidi North

Fill in the blank

The midnight noise is only bothersome to [insert your name]
but to [insert name of another person]

it reminds them of [choose one] bonfires / summer
sacrifice for rain / the hooves of the black horse with white legs

To you it brings back horrible memories of [insert horrible
yet common experience]

Imagine for example you are a [insert name of favourite animal]
and you happen to hear the sound of [insert name of slightly more
aggressive animal]

and you're frightened of [vivid description of said animal's said noise]
maybe you [insert thing animal does to survive]

I'm telling you, next time you hear the midnight
noise you won't panic. You'll fill in the blank

Holly H. Bercusson

no fat saints

beneath a black firmament
I bend out the window
and while my two fingers reach
in my head I recite
the litany of shame:

       [

         [

           [

     [

I repent with each heave
and with each gasp
one more time now
into the mulch below.

before I felt myself ossify
I would walk
for hours I couldn't stay still
body-manic
burning the calories / trial by fire
mortification of the flesh.
a beast that must be broken.
such a good habit,
my neighbour remarked.

Saint Catherine of Sienna said it:
build a cell in your mind.
food is a distraction
I tell myself
but I know
nothing waits for me at the end.

Iain Britton

Deep down the air is rarely sweet

i've given up being particular
about who's coming to visit   who's there to stare at me in the dark
who wants to see a man with his reproductive equipment on show
raw & retracted   a man who feels with his hands
with his eyes switched on in the sunless cellblock of his head

no point he reckons guessing who's coming for breakfast for lunch
or dinner   no point in worrying about fucking etiquette
or presentation   or how one looks   or how one ought to look

deep down the air is rarely sweet
i live here with my brother
i live here because one day
the rock on which we once stood opened its jaws & swallowed us

swallowed some other jerks too

no one yet has lifted the rock to let us out
no lightning flash of wings to check how we are
or where we are   there've been no Marys (if you know
what i mean) no apparitions of famous females
no saints' stairway to heaven
          as if we need it

all i have is my brother (when i see him) & myself
sharing mouthfuls of yellow water
which ooze from the hills
slime which leaches through rocks
juices of the dead which leak from above

now's not the time to visit   now's not right with the electro-magnetic
field   the tectonic plates are on the move   you scratch my gold dust

& i'll scratch yours   the mine's arteries are cracking up
the earth's heart keeps having seizures   i have reddish spots
crawling all over my skin

now's not a good time to drop in   there's a manstink here that's
unavoidable   that's not for the tourist the curiously courageous
or speleologist who wants to discover what it's like to breathe
downunder or like Orpheus to come for a while to snoop about
like Rūaumoko without letting off steam

a manstink is what you'll get   is what i'm used to   that speaks
of ages rotten eggs lousy longdrops in strategic places   there's
a pong here from a fallen slaughter

my brother's with me & then he's not   he travels about like a bat
a silent mover   relying on soft sonic tapping   the slightest hints
of change   my brother's a stranger   living at depths where angel-
freaks fear to tread   or even cough   he knows this uterine chaos
of broken-down shafts & rock implosions like the pipes & sewers
of any great city

we live by feeding on long-legged wētā in the dark

i've heard voices now & then
heard children cherubim cupids
the noises of thugs & thieves
lovers copulating
the spill of sperm
of people toileting like cats
dirt bikes doing wheelies
people picnicking
laughter & sobbing
the sounds of storms   the *1812 Overture*   of nature
crashing   i've felt God's feet plodding heavily

the mine shakes its hollowed-out belly   gone the gold
the silver the men with ravaged lungs

i don't believe in 'get down on your knees or else' . . .
i don't believe anyone's listening
i don't believe in holy rollers
in Paradise or Milton as he sees it
i don't believe in born-again hippies on the road to India
in the cardboard ashrams of bearded poets
in wiping the slate clean
in phantasmagoric operas
& all that voodoo stuff

i've got no choice
no choice   my brother & i are stuck
like condemned moles in plugged-up holes

the sun tells us nothing the moon doesn't speak   we read cockroaches
we read them like braille   we touch rocks that shake   touch ledges
overhangs   wooden beams   sometimes the ground feels
as if it's perpetually shifting   we chew on worn-out stories
of what's happening under the family tree or between the floorboards
of our home   we remember the marram grass   the sand dunes
amongst the croaking creeks

i conjure up pictures of received information   i've one of myself
inhabiting the airspace above College Street surviving on starlight
& confessions & fucked-up thoughts   we both admit to succumbing
to flashing moments of childhood   we live for the day   for the
animal who lives within us   the animal who lives by being open-
mouthed & sometimes gorged   i want out   to be propelled upwards

            to spiral & spin   i want to go fast   so fast there's every
likelihood i'll disappear from the endangered list of insects & bats

i stand in darkness listening to the tumbling black sea   a black
formless place where the horizon scratches   where gold-rimmed
clouds gather & a parade of soft lights shows us the door

i stand naked   thinking of a woman's name

I'm writing a poem tonight

I'm writing a poem tonight and it's going to save my life keep me on the road rescue me from falling I'm writing a poem tonight and it's going to set me free from the past cure my ailing mind turn down the volume on this anxiety irrational (isn't all anxiety irrational?)

this poem will answer my questions allay my fears particularly the ones I am feeling right now will keep me company through the long darkening hours banish my loneliness once and for all I can see it solve the riddles which still exist in my head   after nearly 49 years of puzzling and decoding the riddles still riddle   this poem   will be best friend gentle mother constant father a welcome antidote to all the girls who told me to go away who said they didn't want to play this poem will be lover who never confuses is never angry never needs space this poem will be constant will never leave will never misunderstand me what a gift what a revelation how incredible it will be to find all my needs met instantly in a moment, in one small gathering of words on a single page how efficient

and once I've written it can you believe I will feel calm once I've written it I will feel complete my head clear for the first time questions will no longer rage rage rage in   the chest of my heart will not lock me up tight with their bewildering imperceptibility suffocate me with their incessant interrogation will not continue to blast

themselves at me time after time after question after question after question this poem will answer them all.

something to be certain about

we die with weight we can't lose
we die with feeding tubes and no last supper
we die at summer picnics with strawberries and brie
we die at 3am in dark hospitals listening to strangers snore
we die on our way to coffee with a friend, as often as
we die on our trip to Calvary
we die at thirty-two and eighty-seven
we die with chia seeds and Moro bars lining our bowels
we die with a Ferrari or a bus pass
we die single, divorced or happily married, or married
we die unable to decipher everyone's tone
we die content, indifferent or in agony
we die, a certainty, so sway, hands on your head, until you're dead.

Lodestone

I know *the message of the winter*,[1] navigating your death and this
perpetual sadness, and the ways in which grief crouches in wait
with its gnashed teeth and knife eyes, whenever snow crests the
hills in hushed silences.   I restring myself in echoed
duplication, only to loosen the taut bindings with a sharpened
in-breath, for this is nothing like the saltiness of a lover's skin, it
lies thick and ashen on my tongue.

Let me tell you of the ocean's whisper, far beyond the breakers,
and in beckoning surges at my thighs. Let me tell you of the gibbous
moon's promise, hauling me towards glow-worm pin-holed stars,
seeking to illuminate a broken heart.   Shall I run to the
shore with the wind at my back, place my faith in the whenua until
it abates, hoping something will remove my earthbound shackles?

I watch as loneliness shrouds itself in memories I long to escape, air
stilled with apparitions of you at the perimeter. There are no more
ancient rākau to greet, because I remain forever splintered at their
feet.   I cannot neglect the shuddering cries of love
unconstrained, or the elemental wounds exposed to rejecting stares,
for in this dampened manawa there is no answering sky.

I converge in the truths of dark-veined waters, lapping at the spaces
in my intricately scythed chest, like a lodestone in your pocket that
longs to return. Whetū blink cold in the quickening, forsaken
devotion limps itself towards an earthly pause.   There is no
saviour in this wild place, where hollowed cheek confronts the
reddened dust, no secrets in my heart when I kneel hearthside to
my soul, no karakia when hope has vanished in the absence of moonlight.

---

1   'the message of the winter' is from 'Before I Knocked' by Dylan Thomas.

Yet when the cushioned moss underfoot has finally worn away, I will direct my face to the sleeted rain, until I hear your voice again.

My mother's rose bushes

Pruning them back was just the start
soil had to be dug out
on every side

spades placed like levers
under the thorns
leaned on

like Archimedes
time and again
till with a mandrake groan

they gave up the ghost
we hustled them onto the lawn
till I got scared

that they'd somehow
re-root themselves
so shifted them

onto the concrete floor
one looked like a lung
with arteries attached

another like a beating heart
all night I could hear
them scratching

on the windows
wanting to get in
resume their reign

punish the usurpers
the scaffolders will be here
on Wednesday next

and after that other plants
less inimical ones?
will take their place

after the last pit was emptied
Zero the cat
pissed and shat

in the empty hole
as if to confirm
our victory

Fade to Black

Not a bad name for a coffee bar given the espresso and Americano. We order the latter and cradle our cups as the evening fades. With the coffee we savour lovely words: nocturnal, twilight, gloaming, afterglow. We turn aside crepuscular as being vaguely reptilian and all at once both words signal a slight shift in the temperature. There is a coolness now in the air, and with it the coffee cools. The night is fading to black. The Spanish waiter turns on the lights but the black persists. His hair is pulled into a black ponytail. I reach for your hand in the darkness seeking comfort. All is fading, deepening, apart from the waiter's brilliant smile as he comes to the table to ask whether we'd like more.

unWelcome swallows

Where did they come from, these hyperbolic birds
stretching the air's truth in all directions?
My hands grab the brakes as I flinch
at their lowflying wingclips —
the cyclist ahead rides blind, head down,
through avian dogfights.

But who was to know that snivelling clouds
would shower swallows
on two strangers battling an easterly gale,
on this weary town with another sea-storm
blowing snot on its windows.

Little twitterpates, we are many also,
unhoused, unhinged by the cyclone.
Like the burgeoning eaves that ached with your nests
giving way to rising floodwaters,
our bridges have moved out to sea in a mud glacier
of mangled lives.

No doubt weeks of rain have driven us to ride
this concrete river together,
scouring the heavens for signs of hope —
any patch of blue will do it.

Jan Kemp

Chimera — a song cycle

I Eastern Wall

You are my wailing wall — silent, stony, ancient, revered,
& full of crevices where I bury my wishes,
scrawled in darkness & screwed up to stuff into your cracks,
as I mutter them under my breath, praying & nodding,
knowing you won't answer. Never will.

But you hear them.
For these both, I give thanks.
I come face-to-face with myself.

II A chased love

A chaste love, such as Dante's for Beatrice,
Jesus' (we presume) for the Magdalene,
or St Francis' for God,

I can offer you, who outran me from the start,
predicting my path would lead back,
from hands held once in the woods.

I still see no chance of that. Hold
only a chimera of what once was.
This I now breathe out back to you.

But I know, you'll have none of it.
You want only the chase,
the capture, the conquering.

III You silly goose

Let sleeping lovers sleep on —
safer in their own beds than in yours,
less disruptive.
No more turnings over
of old turf, old coals,
however much they glimmer still.

Leave the past, let it lie,
simmer on in the peace & balance
of the present.
You've made yourself a lovely new bed,
with a duvet of duck-down.
Now climb up & lie in it.

IV Pact

I give you back the love you gave,
the love I dare not keep —
we're each embedded in another's life,
from sleep to sleep.

There's nothing left to reap alone,
save these words, daily written out of me,
for you to have & say aloud,
as if they were your own.

I Start to tell You

Sky's violet, Winter moon a stained white plate
so pale it's almost porcelain, the wind is helping
blue gums shake night from their leaves and footprints
follow like kelpies as wellies part wet grasses.

Sock footed and the kitchen's cold. I set a match
to kindling. You used to do that. *When you've fed
the chooks and horses, your porridge will be hot.*
Now oats are unopened, the fire another beast to feed.

Outwith, our hens commence their hesitant polka: peck,
cluck, step, repeat, the chestnut and his friend dip whiskery
noses into chaff, and smiling I turn, start to tell you
about that dove with a horsehair moustache. Remember.

Thunder and three black birds fly South. Lightning flickers
over hills like a faulty fluro. No torch wavers up
from stables with its yellow promise of arrival.
No boots *clump, clump* steps. Rain on tin is white noise.

Picking up specs you left on the dresser, I fold, unfold,
fiddle with your keys, sniff the tobacco tin, tell myself
that love does not stop with loss, dissolve like aspirin.
Tomorrow I know, the world will begin again, be as empty.

Jane Simpson

Imagined scar

Where will you live inside
my new bra?

How high must the cup line be
to hide you from others if not from my self?

Front-fastening muscle memory has me here
again, 26 years on in the fitting room.

At the counter I see it has pockets for the prostheses
I will never need, I say.

The assistant says to keep the receipt and send it off
with the surgeon's note to the Ministry of Health.

Every year the paperwork came
for my mother's new post-surgical bra.

I never saw her scar in life —
the closest, the hour after her death.

Janet Newman

Nocturne
Powelliphanta traversi traversi

Over moss and leaves
your slow weave of star shine.

A possum asleep in the kahikatea
above a litter of empty shells.

Janet Wainscott

'In loving memory'

The white paint in the inscription
on my mother's headstone
is beginning to flake. The *oh*
of loving and the *why* at the end
of memory, all peeling away.
A blank panel waits for my father.

We're more a white paint than gold letters
sort of family; but perhaps even that is a bit gaudy
for Mum. I'd like to pick away the paint, expose
the grooves sandblasted into the smooth, still
shiny granite and read with my fingers.
My father need not know about the paint.

Samhain

They do not care if you perform all the fleshy pleasures; they've seen it all. There are no delights unknown to them, no horrors. If you drown a kitten; the dead are not shocked, though they may be saddened (you should not drown a kitten). There is no shame for you before the dead. They see you and see you and it changes nothing.

The dead want to know what you've been up to lately. They are genuinely interested because not so much is happening with them. If you were thinking of dying, consider this: life has more going on.

On Samhain, the dead come over and sit with you. Some of them are having a party in your kitchen; others are noticing the cobwebs over the bath. You cannot be lonely. You are never lonely because the dead are with you.

The dead are there when you throw up all the ouzo and raspberry you drank at the inter-hostel ball, when you tie ribbons to a fence to protest for peace, when you are wronged at the office, when your lover abandons you, when you heat up a microwave dinner for one. The dead watch Netflix with you while you cry.

You love the dead. The many dead. The schoolfriends, grandparents, favourite singers, the writers, teachers, aunts and uncles, the people you used to love, the people you love still, family, oh god, family.

The dead are mostly benign and want what's best for you. They want to know what music you're listening to these days and when you say Perfume Genius or Reb Fountain or Moses Sumney, they are interested; everything is interesting when you're dead.

The dead enjoyed life. They've moved on, but they still like to look in from time to time. They like to check you're okay (you can't lie to them; they'll know). The dead are still out there. Just beyond.

If you could see the dead, if you could see the dead, you'd see your little nana, she'd hand you that love that was always there like a pebble you can hold tight to. If you could see the dead, you'd see your father and he'd say, Shush, shush, Sweetie-pie, it's okay my darling, and he'd make it alright. Your sister would be like a sister who just grew up ordinarily, like an ordinary person who had an ordinary life.

The dead have regained their vigour. They are all their ages and you can pick the one that suits. They talk in whispers and sometimes in music.

The dead may appear to you as a radish or a letterbox. But when you need them most, they might be elsewhere. Or next to the envelopes but you just can't see them. It's Samhain and the dead are here, right behind the curtain. If you don't look directly, you can sense the curtain twitching. If you try not to listen, you can hear them sigh.

from The Relevance of Berthe Hoola van Nooten

Fleurs, Fruits et Feuillages

We discovered Berthe by accident.
She was standing in the Javanese Gardens,
lacing her fingers between streaked amaranths
and the soft hair petals on soursop stems.

We fed her like a bird, breadcrumbs
from sandwiches, morsels of fruit
while she drew a tumble of vines
in the air. Fruitless, scentless,
and we stayed till the wind shivered us,
shadows shifted us.
Berthe scuffled in leaves,
Don't leave, she said, and retrieved a book,
Fleurs, Fruits et Feuillages
Choisis de l'Ile de Java.

Saraca Declinata

Berthe is tired.
She sits on his couch the colour
of *Saraca declinata*, the sorrowless
tree, and sips a cup of herbal tea.

Berthe sleeps.
In her dreams there are too many shapes.
Cave bats cover her eyes,
leeches suck on her paper skin.

Wake up Berthe,
wake up my dear, you are quite safe here.

Berthe begins to explore
the past, treks to rising temperatures.

Sun falls
in emerald showers. Specimens gleam
on the canopy floor,
fingertips glide through leaves.

Jessica Le Bas

Driving through the night
For S. W. D.

Do you remember how you lifted our babies
in sleep, lay their soft bodies on the back seat

of your blue Vauxhall Cresta — how you polished
that car for hours. We packed them like kittens,

in mountains of blankets my mother knitted,
and pillows. Your mother's feather eiderdown

Do you remember that drive through the night,
me at the wheel, the first week I got my licence,

my ticket out of the house. You came home
from a late shift, and off we went. All the way

to a place we had never been because we had
never been. My eyes on a road wet with rain

till we left the city, chest to the steering wheel
After Kopu the road turned inland; unsealed and

deserted, winding us like a skein of loose yarn,
over the divide, a mountain range that once

promised gold, through broken hills to Hikuai
Headlights picked out trees, scraggly tea tree

on doughy banks. Possums. A cancan chorus
of metal flying off the chassis. My wrists cast

in caution. How you slept. I have no memory
of arriving at Tairua. The night went on, and us

with it, into an astonishing darkness, buoyed
by the sweet smell of baby talc, our hands

deep in bath water, waking blind from nights
of broken sleep, falling in and out of the crazy

days of their childhoods, and ours. Till years later
we found ourselves in heavy traffic, overtaking

at unimaginable speed. Sirens and yellow lines
How the road narrowed. How we lost our way.

Jessica Thornley

Mahuika Takes the Underground

The way you hit the scene, erupted all over, absolved by an uncanny
London heatwave

That was me in your belly, stowaway, little goddess ember ready to
blow

and you thought it was *super-crazy-weird* how you just happened to
find yourself in hidden hot spots, magma chambers full of sweat, joy,
high as tephra, pre-ordained

Boom Box. All You Can Eat. An illegal bar called Garry's

That was the summer the Griffin moved itself into a carpark, made
good on a smouldering crater and the punters, artists and deadbeats
got accidental tans and drank Pimm's unironically 'cos it was so
blimmin' hot

Of course, your mother had warned you in a been-there-done-that
kind of way, but hey, we all forget

Fire doesn't know itself by fire alone

So, you mix with the misfits, lost boys and demi-Gods

Way before pronouns become a thing I show you that fire is rainbow
coloured, that the hottest part of the flame runs blue

You give away body parts, keratin coal, and I smile and weep with
you, because yeah, my girl, I was fond of him too

Night by night we take Shoreditch in a South Pacific ring of fire

That's me snapping in the rafters, messing with electric until the roof caves in and you cross your molten heart and hope to die while Arctic Monkeys teeter on the edge of fame amidst rubble and ash

That's me rumbling through the underground, flowing you home in lava lust fissures that will harden and heal into your most beloved and beautiful scars

I am the blood in your veins, in your tampon
ejected and stashed in a DVD case — *Annie Hall*, your flatmates' maybe?
under a wet and heaving bed because you were
So
Damn
Fire

I am the throb of foetal stories in your cuticles, the urge to scratch, rip, claw yourself into something real, scary as fuck

I am the shift of tectonic plates, the ruptured crust that causes you to sway in front of Black Triptychs and crumple around a searing core

I sit inside you quietly then, a dense shimmering rock to warm your joints while you cry
and as you leave, and the awe seeps out, you ask

Did I eat you or did you eat me?

Jessie Burnette

sets

your hair stays salt-slick legs waxy red & sun-lined
pale beneath the whitewash spin head ached
& ocean-stoned you wait in the
sand for the rest of the
boys rubbing at
raw sandfly
ankles

the bikini bra bleeds lines down your belly in smoky trails
& you think of slug tracks the viscous stick that
glues predators to the spot mash the
shifty inserts till they run
& run

on the drive you're sweat-stuck hot to leather &
skin bass liver-heavy against your lungs the
corner swing that tastes of teeth & rust
you boys are backseat trouble
hooning hills between
the sets

in the morning your eyes are glassed with it the
shushing waves black and flickered you
wait the board cool between your
thighs when you see him
in the shadowed
swelling
gut

then he is there eye tilted to your own
face is oblong dark against the grey
sun the milky pupil he floats

into your palm rubber
cool then
gone

when the uni students leave the pub's all
yours floor spun blind in disco red
pop drop pass the jaeger beat
dance-drunk & full of
dolphins surf ears
water thick the
ocean
hangs

the mattress is scratchy when he climbs
into your bed i love you beautiful girl
why are you being so shallow i
thought you were
different

your heels echo in the lock-shop air the
rise & crash just beyond the rocks
you yawn & shake till the water
bursts warm from your ears
then rub them empty how
have you lost so
much

Corpse Fauna

When did death first become white
doves, peace lilies, relatives in hats,

a body frozen with formaldehyde,
make-up on a doll dressed up for a party,

and not bacteria, flies, beetles, moths —
all the familiars of death?

Within minutes of dying
a *Calliphoridae* fly finds us,

dances naked on our coinless eyelids,
drinks our fluids, lays its eggs,

and cradles us inside its belly,
able to love what is gone.

It bares our taste into the air
as the ghost soil opens its dark mouth:

welcome home welcome home
welcome home.

... from RIVERSPELL31

Outside Julian's cell's south wall, the silver birch leaves weep on the ground. The yellows of the tears spread across the green of the grass. Karen's apple is swathed in gold as she lifts it to a mouth already filled with laughter. A woman one gives one's life to.

Is it wisdom you want? These rocks are riddled with holes. I am reminded that one thought is not another's subjection. Or whether the rock or the hole in it obeys thought. Or washes or weeps through. What? Sea. Sea.

John Tuke

One of those days poetic

It was one of those days poetic/ when the change in the wintery
weather meant I could get out and recharge the lithium/ this time
working in the arms of an old kōwhai tree/ and it was there I saw the kererū
I'd been getting to know/ searching me with its earth-hewn eye/ so chilled/
the young tradie tells me/ so laid back/ again there's the shiny jacket/ again
the shiny white top/ as if the only moda was shiny/ though I did notice
the mottled bush shoulders/ as if trying to tone down all the glam/ while below
someone was asking me about gender/ I think the bird's gender/ but I really
don't know and/ to be honest/ really don't care/ so it was karma when I heard
birdsong/ they/ and as they remained so close/ I felt like a kind of branched
accomplice/ he hoa/ so I'll take that as a gift/ also happening that day/ like
every other day/ there was bold poetry being written/ humans and other
creatures breathing their first/ their last/ songs of joy and songs of lament/
there were opening lines/ stanzas and heart murmurs/ tentatively or
wildly scrawled out in notebooks/ on discarded packaging and the backs
of half-finished love letters/ while about this time we were changing trains on
the subway/ rushing up escalators/ then along never-ending tunnels that gently
followed the curve of the earth without us knowing/ and it was now evening/
in that part of town around East 4th and Lafayette/ where Bowie hailed the taxi/
a clandestine gathering of writers and their colluders/ where I hear words of
myriad colours and scents never before woven/ never pixelled together/ then
after the laying and surrender of these poems/ to the salt breeze
coming in off the sea/ they become bright prayer flags/ breaking away
and drifting through the buildings/ in the city of beautiful teeth and
bleeding gums/ towards Central Park/ where Ada's fillies/
with their huge hearts pounding/ run between the pillars/ seeming
as ancient as the Susquehanna river that flows nearby/ and it is
there/ high in an American elm/ the kererū waits/ looking out for you/
down through the tumbling light/ and the cascading poetry of greens

Eleanor

I once worked in Bunnings with Eleanor Catton
It was basically a Benchmark
Had just been bought out
Capitalism and all that
All the accounts books still read Benchmark
And all the stamps and all the old credit card readers
We had to use that one time when the machines stopped working
Because of computers and Wi-Fi
I think that was invented then

I worked Saturdays
And Sundays
With hangovers each and every day
Employee of the month in May
Once I went straight from town at 6
To work at 7
And slowly came to the realisation
The lunchtime horror
That hot pants were not an acceptable
part of the Bunnings uniform
No one said in words
It was their stares
That told me
When they saw under
That apron
Those tradies' narrowed eyes
And their sun-kissed skin
Smelling of diesel and sweat
I imagined fucking them
In the timber yard
The old men especially
By the bread factory

They offered to fix my door
Of my bedroom
Which I took up
But I was trying to be a good girl then
So it was just putty and sanding
And my box
Of beers I bought

Sheryl was like the grandma to everyone giving us advice
How to start an account and get rid of head lice
Her real name was Margaret but I think she liked John Rowles
And Paul taking everything literally who was the most fun to
antagonise
Murray was all sensible wisdom and serenity
Cass and Zane taking party pills with me
On a Wednesday
Sort of like a family

Eleanor spent time in the office
With the intellectuals
She was kind to me
Like you would be to a puppy
A girl failing uni

Would she remember me?
I was just the girl in hot pants with a hangover
Charlie hit on her
Then was outed as a stalker

Eleanor asked me questions
And laughed at my jokes
You could tell she was clever

And when I read her name in the paper
I was not surprised she had made it
She was like a light shining out of that customer services desk
She could even cut keys
And the bosses liked her too
She wasn't hungover
You could tell
She wouldn't be there long
Now I drive past that spot
On the way to Newtown
It's a Countdown now
Shiny and megalithic
Looming over the intersection
Those timber frames
I imagine
Like sunken treasure in watery depths
Entombed in a hard plastic shell
Those memories of Cody's at the Christmas party
10 min ghosts on smoko
sipping tea and coffee
Eleanor telling me about her student loan
And of the stocktake clickers
I wonder if she thinks about Bunnings ever
And if she based a character on Paul from customer services

Mother as poet

At a safe distance, they
Gawked at her as she
Crept crudely into a cooked life,
I turned three as they unstrapped the
Two of us
From the safe cave,
Her voice
Peals away from rooms like a godhead calling
Me to finish what I'd started,
Life is coming, you must be rehearsed,

Standing at the podium she stares across at me,
Yes you, I wrote this for you, I'm reading this to you,
Write me right away
Speak to them through me
Dearest little boy,

Listen, listen to the telling air
                              I'm exhaling into you,
Do not buckle,
Do not sit meekly in a soulless house
                              with crying as company,

Above all little boy,
Be above it
                as it passes beneath you,
        The curdled river under the brittle bridge.

I wake @ 2am and know

you'll be running home from the university
down the track where ferns clutch your arms
past the basilica an engine of votive candles
waving through the feet of glass saints
even faster past the funeral home with the sad
lantern till you reach your flat pressed into
a bank like marzipan once when you opened
the front door there was a wild pigeon in the hallway
beak wide eyes wider to see you and where it had
pecked worried begged the windows shards
and shards of blood

La Sylphide

The mist evaporates
off the hills
three spiders have an orgy
in a corner I can't reach.
Synergy can't compete
with synecdoche.

Every two weeks
transform into a sylph
the night is young —
nearly a full pack
of Pall Malls awaits.

Always pause
in your driveway
to apply lipstick
of dusty pink particles.

It's nice to say
'I love you' again
even if I'm not sure
I mean it.

Let's complete
repetitive mandalas

Pause again
in your driveway
to scull my drink
stash the evidence
in the glove box
then 2 breath mints
to disguise the vapour.

Only your dog knows.

a love poem

it's mid-winter darling
    the window frames are swollen & furry

water runs our insides
    & when we're drained
    the liquid is gray
    & stains the sink

        this is a love poem
        but we're very   tired

    of the same bills
    for the same amounts
    that always catch us
        in the same ribs you'd tattoo
were it ever possible to get some fucking time off work

it's a love poem
    in which we are both looking older
but it's probably just from stress
    that cannot be undone

        a love poem
        where we never marry
            & the children we have are beautiful
        because they take solely from you

the cold comes in
    through gaps   we cannot see
but my knees your womb   our cyclical throats   & noses
know well enough
to charge the ache   rent

or at least ask it
to wipe the skirting boards
once in a   blue   moon
it's got something to do with
things being built of shitty MDF
before we knew how to write love poems
that meet healthy homes
& come out different than this

we're approaching the age of suicides my darling
& I'm hoping you'll stay   & dance
over tape measures
the landlords use
to size up our carpet
while we haggle on how to best split
the cost of melatonin

even though   I never remember
to wipe the stove-top
'cos I've spent my mental headroom
on quotes from *Barton Fink*

stay even though
the sex I might've otherwise disappointed you with
is bludgeoned out of us
come the end of the working week
& the fumes I'm running on
are the ones that make you ill

stay so I can read you
a love poem
about wanting to rock your god body

were it not for an early zoom

it's a love poem
    a love poem
    this is love
    & I worry sometimes
love can be made to look like the rest of life
        when we aren't looking

a love poem
in which schedules have rendered
us long distance   despite sharing an address

    a love poem stuck in traffic
    & I'm one unwoffed car
            in a sea of unwoffed cars
    on Wairere
            & now I'm free
    I can't think of the happy bits

    & I told you I'd only write one
            after you leave
    because what's the point
    in words
            if they aren't the last ones

but this isn't that
        & you'll just have to trust
this is a love poem
                even if we're sometimes strangers
                                in it

            just as home is still home
    even if it's sodden
& cheap

& sleepless shivering
    in separate beds

      a love poem where it's all slow moving
  but too quick just the same
& the years tick off us
like bad atoms
    & that dryer Dad gave me
    has our clothes smelling of cat piss

it's a love poem where I hope
    you're with me 'til I die
    & that you never do
        a love poem where sometimes I don't hear you
        because the wind's howling indoors
        & other times because I'm not listening

a love poem where I wake you after lights-out
because I sprint up the stairs on all fours
    like a grey   hound

  it's a love poem
where the noise of love
    is a sigh
& whatever you're not watching on tv

but it is a love poem
   & there's nothing I wouldn't give
        to be bored
    & daily ground to near dust
         with you

      because between it all
      too small to see

with the dinner plates I have for eyes
that the dishwasher can't be arsed to clean
are moments
we're laughing
about how piteous this all is
& were it not for you
I wouldn't see the funny side
of any of it

Liz Breslin

In Kathmandu, Te Tihi-o-Maru

Note: no actual lesbians were harmed in the making of this poem

the word mannequin means little man
but these two are definitely lesbians
and all we are trying to do is
make them hold hands

when i say we i mean i
am leaving this to Eliana
because of the skill-saw hacking
of my middle right finger

and none of the nurses were like
              o no your middle right finger
which is proof that they were not lesbians
or at least not right-handed lesbians

Eli is twisting the hand
of the activewear-wearing lesbian
with no hair towards the hand
of the slightly taller double-rolled outdoor pant

wearing lesbian with no hair
we are nearly there
we are nearly there
we are nearly nearly

queer joy tramping angels singing
their fingers almost touching
Eli twists the hand of the outdoor
lesbian towards the outstretched now

hand of the activewear lesbian and
her hand pops off in their hand
we are twisting our faces in contortations
jesus

fuck
we have broken the lesbians
we have broken the lesbians
Eli places the guilt

filled
fiberglass
lesbian
hand on the corner of the display and we don't look back

later at Caroline Bay they will
hold my bandaged right
hand above the water
while i put the rest of me under

Pastoral Leakages

You can't stand in the same river twice
You can't measure an algal bloom by how verdant
it appears at midnight — that would be selling it short.
Here is what we can do:
sit in thoughtful silence in an upturned Toyota Hilux
row a boat down a shopping cart crowded canal
and sing out *Hello, Amsterdam!* to a field of confused horses.
You can feed ducks pages from your diary
and then drive those ducks to market
with a pail of water over each of your shoulders,
and a pebble in your shoe
to show you have tenacity.
There's no telling whether this town is big enough
for two of anything —
there's only one road in and out
and even that is a strain.

Good Weather for Ducks

All that birdseed, and the rain,
The ducklings,
Running in the house,
Falling over our hands,
Splashing fluff and soft, wet feet,
Didn't help us in the end.

The birds didn't warn us,
They didn't knock twice,
On the window,
And say, get out,
You've stayed too long.

The rain's in my head now,
I hear it in the library,
Or standing in the street,
And I think,
Spare the jonquils,
Leave us the jonquils.

And the rain in your eyes,
Makes nothing glisten,
It just falls,
On the apple trees,
On the broken asphalt,
On your tea in the morning,
Because the cracked cup,
Your favourite, is gone.

And I miss the old rain,
That made you smile and say:
Good weather for ducks.

Margaret Moores

Likeness

(Diego Velázquez: Las Meninas*)*

I: The artist

Perhaps you knew Velázquez once — he has taken a step back from his canvas and his eyes have caught yours. A half-smile. On the wall behind him, a large mirror — if you move a little, the reflection will change, but for now you see two blurred figures. To his left, a sumptuously dressed small blond girl surrounded by her entourage — two meninas, two dwarfs, a chaperone, a bodyguard, a dog. Behind him, a man on stairs leading to a lighted space.

You don't know who you are, or what you are doing.[1]

II: Vanishing points

The elbow of José Nieto, backlit in a doorway by bright daylight — he is turning to leave, or beginning to arrive, one foot on an upper step. Two half-figures glimmering in a mirror beneath red drapery — Philip IV of Spain and his niece-wife Mariana of Austria. Their daughter, the Infanta Margarita Teresa — dandelion fluff hair pinned back with a flowery ribbon. This book of reproductions is heavy. You slide it across your desk and gaze over roofs and treetops toward Waiheke Island. The little orange ferry skims above the horizon. Imagine the ocean as a plate with the islands of the Hauraki Gulf decorating its rim.

Think of a pencil bending in a glass of water.

---

1 'You don't know who you are, or what you are doing' is derived from Michel Foucault's book *The Order of Things: An archaeology of the human sciences*, which begins with an analysis of the Velázquez painting *Las Meninas*.

III: Illumination

A shaft of sunlight from a recessed window illuminates the cheekbone of Mari Bárbola and the collar of Nicolás Pertusato. Achondroplastic dwarfism. Light shimmers on the forehead and bodice of the Infanta — a five-year-old bound into a cream brocade corset, delicate ruched sleeves trimmed in black, a panniered skirt. It brightens the white silk sleeves of the menina, Doña Maria Agustina, allows for a dull glimmer from the King and Queen reflected in the mirror behind the easel, highlights the ferule and bristles of the artist's paintbrush, his palette, the folds of his sleeve.

You have come into this room unannounced and intruded on a family not your own.

Never stare at people who do not look like yourself.

Fondle the dog instead.

IV: Red

The artist's brush is poised over a pool of red pigment — red lake, vermilion and red ochre.

The stockings of Nicolasito, the ribbon at the wrist of the curtseying Doña Isabel de Velasco, the hair adornment of the Infanta and the decoration pinned to her bodice. The scented earthenware búcaro on a silver tray offered to the Infanta by the kneeling Doña Maria Agustina.

Up close, knots in the canvas and splashes of red ochre overlaid with a wisp of lead white, a slash of bone black. Step back and the red brushstrokes on the bodice of the Infanta become a rosette of silk ribbon and beaded lace.

Picture the women of the royal family as soluble, ethereal. Mirages. Imagine them instructing the Infanta to nibble the rim of the búcaro as if it were an ice cream cone because the clay will lighten her skin.

Your red nightgown drips across white sheets.

V: The Infanta as porcelain doll in presentation box

Misidentified as her older half-sister Maria Teresa in eighteenth-century catalogues. Left cheek shows signs of repainting. Eyes move. Head turns. Bodice boned and skirts held wide by farthingale in the Spanish style. Right hand moulded to grasp búcaro (included). Hair can be brushed.

Certificate of Inbreeding: Born in 1651 to the niece-wife of Philip IV of Spain, married at fifteen to her mother's brother — the Holy Roman Emperor, Leopold I. She calls him Uncle. He calls her Gretl. Seven pregnancies, one daughter. Dead in 1673, four months pregnant with a son.

You had a doll like Margarita Teresa once. When you undressed her, you found that her body was filled with sawdust and without her gown she could not stand up. You laid her back in the box, eyes closed as if in a glass coffin. When the little red búcaro went missing, you gave her a posy of paper flowers in its place.

Her empty hand, the swivelling eyes.

worm theory

I

who rolled the ball that never stops? the perpetual sop
that winds us up. i hear the tic toc, break, drop its load
springs, the intricate mess bodies make, a rip as of linen
& they're finished; digested, mixed
in the underlayers of their darkness & bro! we were close
& you look me up like you don't know me?
remember me.

II

how it ends is not important.
it never ends. you only think it does
& there's no beginning, only the middle
so if the picture's lost, & you're lost
unavailable, sucking your finger,
it's the mind & the body's elsewhere,
at the post shop, standing on the corner
at home, the crime scene, polishing
the steak knife, straightening the sheet
on your knees scrubbing the wine stain
off the carpet.

III

i am dry 2 days, slip into idiocy like sleep, dream
that i'm you, cross the street for no reason. dodge
buses, air traffic, pedestrians. fail to make contact
cut the party line, the atmosphere, ignore
leafleteers. i'm going home, uninterested,
in tears, crack on the pavement, scavengers

shit kickers. when i'm on the 9th floor, i live.
i can do anything, quick. i can sing. make you feel
like i'm behind you. over the moon. i can reach you.

i can teach you. be gentle. thumb your shoulders
when you're mad, when you talk with your mouth full
in the bathroom; when you're fried on the bed with the nets
wide open.

all of this is possible, a blast at the mindscapes
we cultivate. i'm still dreaming, not listening.
not hearing la la.

IV

i said i'd stop but kept going. rolling over,
not dead, the same ground but different.
have you noticed the infinite variation, the sly
nuance of word, facials, blades of grass, leaves
on their stems, how they resemble when it's winter
desiccated bodies.

i'm grafted to myself & tell you about it
in electronic letters.

V

bodies spill.
swarms, systems so good
majority rule, dictatorship. the end of the neo-liberal
emporium. save us jesus, america.

i shake the withered fig tree, but nothing
no future, but this, strung between two twigs
the instant miracle.

VI

god loves the suicides as much as us,
for their courage, their weakness.
god loves the unblessed, the haters
for their suffering. loves them indiscriminately
w/out blinking. god loves those who help themselves
like there was no such thing as possessions.
god loves all the trees & all the animals.
god loves but can't do anything for me.
i love them for that. their impotence, their humanity.

for the dead there's nothing but regret
but what's that?

VII

it's only curiosity that makes me think about jumping off the bridge.
to see what happens next. what i think when i hit the water.
that's all it is. i tell you, i am joyful. uplifted. i connect, am part of
the organic cosmic furniture (of things). i fit, wing it like birds
flit, fleshed in the palpitations of the corporeal soil, renascent red
white & blue, blood oranges & emerald.

give me peaches, conical clusters, wasp nests, the fruits
at the end of summer, joyous flies & the first grapes
of the dying year. this is no time to think of death, to meditate
our beginnings & ends, but to hold the inordinate weight
of sunlight, the intermittent click of consciousness, cicadas
on the blink. at night the crickets are thinking.

VIII

i crossed the arabian desert; saw the confluence of two rivers
serpents; isis, black beetles, water carriers; here is where
i reckon the first Man exited africa, a garden we killed in
were dis-assembled in. there was no such thing as happiness,

doubt, emotional insecurity. then lunch was served & the monotony
broken.

when i got to the heart of western christianity,
i was done, dissatisfied, had i come for nothing, for the roman
taxi driver — may his jewels roast in the eternal pit
sink in cocytus, that unscrupulous heartless bastard —
charged high prices. actually, that time, my cousin picked me up
from the airport, drove us thru the scorched roads of latium
until we reached the taciturn sabine countryside, a reclusive
paradise of rock, high woodlands. francis lived here, conferred
with birds, beasts of the fields. i lived here, dream of it, wolves
of your childhood, the crows, owls that signify death, someone close.
i'm torn; here again, i trudge thru the snow in my old boots, & a gun
that won't shoot / straight.

Wairēinga/Bridal Veil Falls

This is some descent,
steps spilling into the earth
past hordes of passionflower,
maidenhair, spider orchids'
tongues probing floral sinkholes.
I'm agape at these sieved waters,
blotting dark spirits
with ballet-length tulle,
shifting over a face braced
by cowardice and courage;
exiled between this underworld
and the far-fetched
as guardians hold her
upright, draw her eyes back
to the leaping off point
where clouds pass in jousting light.
Being both real and not real,
she punctures this place,
gaze lowered with intent
to take flight before little death
and the conjugal night,
to leave the veil where it falls,
fulling its chasmic pool,
move through aisles of rush
and meadowsweet, seize silver gilt
hanging in baskets under the cladic bees,
languish in dogrose,
the wide open on its knees.

In the Midnight Zone

night fell and never got up
so many floors of sediment ago
the sun forgot all signposts
as the rainbow sank past the last bar
of reception, nightshade
photons relinquishing blue.

valleys under perpetual winter
play their sea scales of silence
only woken by eldritch howls
from upstairs neighbours, gales
pounded to gibberish
down the towering stairwells.

with no outdoors, all is interior
water and bodies plasticine
each other in the black suspense
of eternal afternoons
scribbling notes on a tomb
that say yes even here

never seen yet see-through
eyes swim in skull globes
pocketing the basics
on blackout rations and no telling
how heart-in-mouth they savour
the luminous sherbet of another.

Michael Giacon

The kiss of light

Belluno '87

1. A buried pulse sounds somehow
tracking home through moist murmur
lovers on stairs in shadow. My head
is faces with foreign tongues
I tell them all about me, basically
I — a m — n o t — f r o m — h e r e
but in shade, the same adorning
the girls and boys I see a sudden face
turn — the pool and the soldier lingering
in the changing room — an arm of blue
light takes the camouflage for a mirror
two strangers strange in a town
of crowded night.

2. Back at the polished surface I shut
out tomorrow's sun to cancel the sound
of morning and take my pulse in words
per line that talk for us dark youth.
I give the cousins old words
for my new world dream and haunt
their town, corners kissed warm
by daughters and sons hidden yet holy
their romance no crime.

3. A room tight with fluorescent light
whereby language anointed I multiply
tomorrow less foreign, more me.
Her beauty was made for the shade outside
my student with lips beyond gloss
eyes more dark than dark words.

Like a toy after torture or heaven in hell
white light etches this shape of desire
as a choice between pleasure and pain
     l'ultimo, spegni le luci
last one out, turn off the lights — it's me
straight with faces, fluorescent with duty
down to the coupled town, kissed catcalls
shading my passion with solitude.

4. In the language of love our need is a cause
dark twin. Before we're buried by separation
let's kiss a complacent shadow strange, heads
twisted to senseless shapes but eyes for the light.
I walk to the beat of a hiding heart, he who takes
the long way there who lingered by a vacant
corner hot with the taste, tense for the touch
of a shadow, unbuttoned.

Strains: Northern Lights

Newmarket is always a blur after midnight,
but tonight these preternatural lumens
are competing against each other.
There's the cold LED glare of shop windows
with their empty perfumes and watch
trays lit behind latticed iron security bars,
the steady imperceptible strobing
of the fluoro sign outside the Malaysian joint,
the hyper-pixelated show reels
of corporations trapping in digital
on the bones of last century's billboards.
Diodes, capacitors, rectifiers and transistors
bridge the circuits in a city of memory.
Never again will I find that room
where heads came from all over the city
to share the gospel of weed and hip-hop,
and a sesh that stopped me checking out early.
The Stoics have told us that the past
belongs to death, so I burn my offering
in the flash new carpark building
that stands on the site of that shitty flat
and the room we smoked out like a temple.
My body is also a city of memory.
One day it will belong to the past as well,
but tonight it still belongs to my senses,
to this amulet of dank flower,
and the prayer of thanks I utter here
for its years of guidance and persistence.
Somewhere, up above all this, the moon
and stars are trying to get their two cents in.

Nathaniel Calhoun

blue penguins

our beach afternoon:
five blue penguins dead

small in the seaweed
one of them gutted

a sixth heaves itself
from the dropping tide

toward unsurvivable night.
when you have the option

in your weariness
at least not to drown —

even if your life
has loved the sea —
you take it.

if this text chain finds you,
send something back:
After Adrienne Rich

> bits of skin punched out of your lobes after searching *which ear is the gay ear?*

> crescent clippings from your middle & ring fingers

> her yellowed shoelace tied around your wrist in place of promise rings

> notes tucked away in paper chatterboxes, graphite smeared from sweat tipped hands fold/
            ing & un/

                  fold/

                              ing

> white plastic lollipop stick licked down to the bone, the only kisses you could share in public

> candid polaroid at a party with the two of you violet hued in beanbags, her hand on your thigh; historians will say you were a pair of *really good friends*

> valentine's day cards with fake 'boy' names so your parents don't start asking the wrong questions like *aren't you getting too old to share the same bed, dear*

> a grainy nokia picture of her face creased petal from your pillowcase

> your art deco library card forgotten in her copy of sarah waters' *tipping the velvet*

> collar of your uniform blouse striated red, fossilised memory of when you tried on her mother's lipsticks in the upstairs bathroom while her parents were out

> palm-sized rock she brought back for you from her family vacation
to coromandel; she said *it looks like a heart* and you snorted *no
it doesn't* and she said *it's anatomically correct and that's better
because it's real*

if this text chain finds you, send something back so i know we're real.

Nicholas Wright

The Firebox

In time you think left alone in a house
you might be made natal to its knowledge
simply by way of occupation become
agreeable inside its years of settlement
cognate with the ways others inhabit it;
of course, you know it will never be yours.
The Oregon rafters bow, the cedar
and tin knock and tick to heat and to cool
and always in the valley of their saying
the choking cock's crow, or a horse on the road
and other passers-by somehow inside
the rooms, returning at corners to surprise
you, hearing the thoughts of your neighbour
bending deep in her garden, the great congenial bowl
of her in which children passed and theirs began.
But here, now and new: *a strong gauze of sound*
high-pitched and haunted, its edges feathered to rags
inside the firebox where large spring flies
in their too-many have made their way
down the flue to the shroud of jellied waste
a winter's act of making, nothing, cast
carelessly in the box for burning.
I see them. The hiving, rust-fringed bodies
colliding, now and then, taking after
each other; the excitement of beginnings just
this other side of the glass, and with them
a nest of pencilled pages, twigs, a twist
of fronds and perhaps there's only one thing
to do, though you know, of course you do
were your hand to enter, the flies would take it.

Nicola Andrews

Now that Dr Ropata is in Guatemala

Hone reckons the coffee's better here, shade-grown at altitude,
mineral-rich. He knows better now, shudders at the memory of
Nescafé dregs forming constellations around luke-warm Arcoroc.
There are nights that stretch wide open, watching the futsal with a
cold one, eyeing up the girls at the bar. They fancy him for a Mestizo,
until he opens his mouth. Shrieking with laughter, they pull him
onto the dancefloor where his footsteps falter among marimba
melodies. Cheeks burning, he realises his credentials impress no one.
They do things differently, here. On most nights, he hunches over
the dictionary, sounding out Español. Flash cards rise and recede,
tidepooling the words for *operation, fever, malignant, transfusion,
please.* On his lunch breaks he overpays for plantains and black
beans, fights a craving for kōura. He eats alone, feels too far from the
sea. He spends a day admiring Mayan taonga at the museum and is
overwhelmed by invisibility. It's quite possible that no one in this
entire country could place his homeland on a map. Later, he sends
a postcard to Gizzy, for his cousin's 21st. There's a whole planet out
there, you know; and much that needs to be done. He considers it:
How much good he could do, and who for, and when. And where.

a kind of agony

they are watching TV, itself
a kind of agony, where every
character talks in such a way,

then does it in some other,
with someone else, and he
has his feet up against her

thigh, arches, wriggles toes
that's all, he allows nothing
more than that affectation;

so comes to her a memory,
threshold to a woman's room
incense-warm and lit low

enough for fever, intensity
an inclination, a denudation
of a desire to be embalmed

sweet-oiled, for eternity
but blindfolded by her plight
and, so quiet, she slips into

the future with her squirming
swag of stolen memories,
emerges bound to ancient

anticlimax; walked over once
again, subscribes to tears,
that primal streaming service

Olivia Macassey

Millstone

If I were younger when I said I blight the lives
of all I touch, it would sound like harmless theatrics/
debauchery/ lovers' cruelties/ something to do
with adolescent politics/ sad bois/ cutters/ petty arson;
and now I'm middle-aged and can't
afford shoes, it probably sounds like harmful theatrics/
gambling debts/ spousal abuse/ workplace psychopathy/
machiavellian politics/ sustained alcoholism/ grandiose
arson for insurance fraud

(but a whimper blight a slow sapping this is what it is to carry me on
your back put food in my mouth carry me on your back while no one
meets your eyes carry me around your neck carry me on your back
we don't say invalid any more

Owen Bullock

Possibles

walking after sickness
a butterfly stops
in front of me
as if to say
you'll be a butterfly again

*

in the pouring rain
under a clear umbrella
he stops reading
wraps the book in a plastic bag
takes a swig from the bottle

*

my son chips in
we laugh at the quote
my daughter
in the highchair says
I don't get the reference

*

the blindman selling
ice-cream from a cart
playing 'Greensleeves'
on repeat
taps his foot to the rhythm

*

an elderly couple
reads the newspapers . . .
occasionally
they comment
and nod to each other

*

are you still happy
with the way things are?
she asks
packing up the camp
in torrential rain

If you have ever had a delayed flight which has meant you've had to run along the painted green line between the Auckland domestic airport terminal and the Auckland international airport terminal — or vice versa — feeling like your legs aren't your own because they can barely function after you've been seated on a flight for somewhere between one hour and fourteen hours, while the wheels on your suitcase(s) struggle to keep up with your pace and the terrain . . .

. . . know that I'm running towards you

and I run run run run run run run run through the night and why isn't this bit better lit I can't quite see the green line is the turn-y bit here I think I turn here oh no that wasn't the turn-y bit okay okay I'll just climb over this low chain fence and it'll be fine run run run run run

and I run run run run run run run run why won't these people move to one side and let me past argh it must be lovely not to be stressed about missing your flight you bastards here I go swerving around you run run run run run

and I run run run run run run run run through this berry-scented vape cloud surrounding the rest area run run run run run

and I run run run run run run run run past all the car rental places run run run run run

and I run run run run run run run run through the rain because it's
Auckland so there's usually rain and have they used some kind of
anti-slip coating on this pathway because surely I'm not the only
person who's had to run this and these shoes don't have good grip
and shit no it's a bit slippery I'm fine I'm fine let's just go a little bit
slower fast walk fast walk fast walk fast walk fast walk

and I run run run run run run run run through a summer's day and
why is Auckland so fucking humid I'm wearing too many clothes
should I stop for a second to take off this shirt how long will it take
me to take off this shirt can I afford to lose that bit of time fuck no
gotta keep going because my flight is due to leave in twelve minutes
run run run run run

and I run run run run run run run run through every movie scene
where one of the main characters has realised they can't live without
your love and they're about to miss their last possible chance to tell
you that and to be happy and so we all, all us movie characters, all of
us afraid to be loveless for the rest of our lives, all of us afraid we're
about to miss our one chance, we all run run run run run

Graveyard Lover

Tonight I came home from the graveyard
1:52 in the morning.
You had asked to talk for a while,
to hold hands through the grass.

Dirt making a home beneath fingernails,
worms wrapped like wedding rings
round your fingers.

The cigarette light that kept us warm,
that had you ignoring the stars behind me.

I said I had to go, took the long way home,
forgot to leave flowers at your bed.

You fell asleep on blankets made of dirt today
so I lay on the carpet till mine felt clean again.

Do you remember lying here with me?
Spine to tile, wood to cheek.
Breath competing with the hum of the fridge.

The rain turned to thunder before the key could unlock
and I thought I saw you,
through stained-glass blur,
on the wooden chair in the kitchen.

The worms sleeping in your hair, now
curled up behind your eyeballs, now
my wedding ring on your finger, still.

I thought I saw you
holding the dress you wore
when they closed the coffin

Slow-dancing
all alone
under the yellow eyes
of the kitchen light

Only you were
    alive, alive,
        alive.

Anastomosis

Summer was here when our soft soles
began to harden from barefooting
on buffalo grass, concrete, hot tarmac,
broken shells and the black scoria reef.
Wet as water rats we raced corks
in the rivulets that flowed from rockpools
as the tide ebbed, built and busted
dams in storm-water drains, slipped
on yellow skins of mud as we dug
in the sloughs of the new subdivision
after rain.
                        At the zoo we realised
the power of darkness and learned
how to disappear. The inspiration
came from neither one of us alone
but from our mutual influence.
Waiting in the artificial night
inside the kiwi house for our eyes
to adjust we held two fingers
in the faces of the adults
as they entered blind from sunlight.
A perfect self-acquitting insult.
Victory on our side, on the other,
well, we couldn't quite say but we knew
it was a gross revolt.
                        We were born
within a fortnight on the same ward
but met only on our first morning at school.
Your mother had told you to find
a kid your age and ask to be their friend,
and from that point we cleaved together till
whatever marks the end of mergings
of that kind

which surely couldn't be
as random as the last time we met up
— the only time since leaving school
because we assumed there'd be plenty
of chances, not realising how far risk
already drew you one way and pushed me
another. That day you appeared
unexpectedly not unexpectedly encased
in mud-caked jeans, and told me how
you'd gate-crashed someone's party,
waking the next morning on the verge
to find an unknown hand had shaved
half your moustache.
                          Our twenties
followed, during which I found more
unadventurous ways of going wrong
while you careered off-road: drugs,
alcohol, a white-water marriage,
a new start in Australia, jobs picked up
and ditched
                  before your final
long deliberate literal losing
of direction in the backcountry
carrying it all until you found
a trickle in the clay beside a slow
anastomosing creek where you
could let it drain away at last,
all of it and you with it, soaking
into drying ground.
                          I think of you
where I can't see you now, in darkness,
holding up two fingers, though
I can't say which way round.

Mild

lie
still
spread eagled
a dissected
Leonardo da Vinci starfish
and puddle beneath the mill

damp, discarded husk

caught to your rock
bed by the clench of
occipitalis
temporalis
masseter
fists

look
you're a dandelion
bent too far
dehydrated
damned

a soft lump of kneaded dough
bulges in the bowl of your pelvis
a concrete trickle
fuses your spine
in grit

cut your bristles
with the soft crunch
of earth beneath your neck
(bent further than it should've)

shake sediment in your eyes
and sever their connection

impaired cognition is the bloodless way to say
the world becomes two dimensional
as if lit by moonlight
flat and colourless
a black door
closed
without a key

when they said that witches melt in storms
was it the slow softening of muscles
once they were tied down?

Do you exist in the fog?
Beyond the doctor's headlights
as he hurries and hurries?

Will you loom up out of the grey?
airless lungs beating
body plastered to asphalt
one wing flapping?

No.
He will tilt your chin up to see if it will click
grind your spine between his hands
and protest that he was only
resting a palm on your forehead.

Now,
lie damp and heaving
beneath the slate
fog covering
a river full of dead things
that wandered where they shouldn't
spoke when they shouldn't
and were swept away

now
lure them with a painted mask
eyebrows on point
smile stamped lips
self-simulacrum
concussion

Riemke Ensing

This is not goodbye
For Eion Stevens

'Not fare well,
But fare forward, voyagers.'
— T. S. Eliot, 'The Dry Salvages'

This is definitely not goodbye, Eion,
even if that might be you waving
in that 1991 painting Kevin wrote about
in *Painted Poems.*

You gave me *a place to sit*
so I'm finding you a place in the ocean you loved.
I've found the perfect spot

on the threshold, look, between gently lifting waves
in the distance
where the sun glints as if making a small pool
for you to float and imagine
yourself drifting towards a horizon
hinting at gold.
Why do I hear Leonard Cohen?

The sky seems to be waiting — that still point
to inner freedom — touching the blue
you embraced from the beginning.

Later, stars will continue to tell your stories.

road kill

blood pacts like death drips
and
trip down the white pebble path behind your house
hold your breath for the sting
break the skin seal in the car home
let the dirt in
cause you're bored
counting the
roadkill
tabby with its guts all out
one
duck with a broken neck
two . . .

we were children who held conch shells
to our ears with the promise of crashing waters
and fine sand beaches
you were a kid
with blue tack stuck in your hair
stuck in the carpet
in your mouth
chewing it like gum
whose lips turn in the theatre between curtain fall
as the set shifts
the throat clearing
sniffles break the silence
vibrations through the seats when you laugh
we immortalised ourselves in the drying concrete pool
that secured the green lamp post outside
that was the autumn your father's boat sank
and suddenly you weren't at arm's length anymore
not walking distance either

I dreamt you drove off the cliffs edge once
tyres hit a bump
some trap between the street lights
a german shepherd for your count
three

Angel Parking

the angels park outside the church on
Saturday evening, the sun melting into the sky
like a pat of margarine while the heavenly
host unload their vehicles two by two

I'm dreaming through
the window and the angels are playing
chess in the parking lot with their instrument
cases on their knees

they'll be waiting when it's time
to take you away

I pack the sun into the margarine tin and
put it in the fridge for the morning; tomorrow
two workmen will come and replace the angel parking sign
with something secular

the church is a home now, but there are still
curls of white down like snowflakes
in the gutters, feathers and ashes
f e a t h e r s and a s h e s

Autumn (onset)

the way the lights are slightly brighter
than you care for
at the table, with a chill grey gathering
in place of skin
   (there are leaves, but you won't always
   stop to watch them falling)
stirring your torpor
round and round
in a smooth white coffee-mug.

heat is an island — though never in the summer —
and today you'll shift from shore to shore
rediscovering
such small and unimportant truths
   (the sky is clear enough to think you'd feel
   ice tumble from the stars)
today, the mass of a blanket
settles on your ribs
with the new-found weight
               of sunset.

[in-flight meal]

you move as a body inside a body
you cut through air from sunrise to sunrise.
keep the windows open, the lights all turned off —
in case you don't make it.
in case you have to run *through* smoke
or run *into* open waters.

the nearest exit is the one furthest away from home.

but there are eggs (scrambled) bread (not toasted)
vodka (neat) and your soft, soft organs
plummeting
all   at   once.
then belly-bang under your feet.
aluminium crack. rubber-burn screech. rest.

ladies and gentlemen, welcome to where home isn't. the local time is
sunrise again.

Sophia Wilson

Do not step here, Othello

scrawled across the broken floor

do not fall through to
spaces beneath our living

I apply lipstick
brighten my visage's porch
please step here

disguising fissures
through which
love disappears

deceived or pretending
our housed, free condition
was given up long ago

seals and symbols shipwrecked
on the teeth of lending traitors
who eat us hungrily, then belch us

who is the captain's captain?
our house is an allegorical lament
dismantled by slow borer

I like my mirrors smeared and misty
beneath errors of the moon
your stony tears pockmark my skin

our treasury is rusted tins, stale spice
flour in which the weevils hatch
another gruesome anniversary

the star-crossed seasons are tragic loss
we are a stewing sea of frail vows

and I am no sweet passage

Sophie Rae-Jordan

Offering

I remember the trees offering themselves
sporadically in the wind:
thrashing, unsettled, evergreen. Those nights

in the crowd, the heat, I felt you searching
for me between throbbing knots of air.
Beating, we lay in the undergrowth, branches

heaving overhead, lagging, barely
balanced on bare feet. We had spent three days
remote, unmoored amongst static

swimming in the earthen river,
cold as stone,
to clean. Three nights

finding each other out
for a second time. I slept barely,
we lay on the ground,

and I searched for some steadiness in it.
It was as if there was a current and you
had set me into it, delivering my weight

like an offering to the water,
braiding itself toward some sea
while I unbraided in it.

Red Hands Cave

After photographing the kangaroos
you take the short, directed walk.
Small creatures scuttle from the path.

Freeze as long as you like
you'll not see them.

It's true the rocks give off an atmosphere
but alien ironwork fronts the cave.
You peer through the welded lattice to
the ochre images and try
to place yourself in there; in there
pressing your hand against the wall,
a hand neither red nor black, a hand
that's never gripped cold bars,
or as much as moved a little finger.

Tunmise Adebowale

A Little Grace

I hail from Nigeria's south-west Ile-Ife, where
the dwarf lambs stare out at the
mountainsides for hours.

The heat like a razor,
with no wool to pool for spending.

The farm is a tired place some mornings.
Moves slow like honey.

When Grandpa tells stories of his older brother's death,
sickness spreading like sunlight,
I think of those sheep in the yard.

I wonder if a man from my family
could be gentle enough.

A generation of work-hurt hands
bending to touch the softness of
the bottom of the basin.

A touch like a pull,
like a yearn for a cure,

like reaching out for
your mother in a dream.

If he stuck his hand out in the middle of the night
doused with sick and sweat, would the youngest of the flock

crane its neck from its place in
the pasture and send him off running?

Someplace where boys never die
before their mothers and mornings are

best spent holding wives by their waist,
dying slow deaths,

juicing life with our teeth
at the breakfast table.

Year 13 winner of the *Poetry Aotearoa Yearbook* Student Poetry
Competition

whakarongo ki ngā manu

listen to the birds

kei konā,
te ao o ngā tauiwi.

there,
the world of the non-Māori.

kaua taku ao.
kaua taku ora.

not my world.
not my life.

e kite ana ahau i ngā manu,
e tātākī ana rātou ki ahau,
e whakarongo ana ahau ki a rātou.
he nui ngā waiata rōreka o ēnei
  manu.

I observe the birds,
they chatter to me,
I listen to them.
these birds have many melodious
  songs.

ko taku ao tēnei,
te ao o te taketake.

this is my world,
the world of the indigenous.

tino rerekē ēnei ao,
nā te mea
kāore i te whakarongo nā
ngā tauiwi,
ki ngā manu.

these worlds are different,
because
the non-Māori
do not listen,
to the birds.

e tau ana i roto i ngā rākau,
e pekepeke ana i runga i te whenua,
e topa ana i te hau,
ngā manu me ā rātou karere whai
  tikanga.

perched in the trees,
hopping on the ground,
swooping in the air,
the birds with their pivotal
  messages.

ko te ao pono tēnei.
whakarongo ki ngā manu.

this is the true world.
listen to the birds.

haumi ē i tā mātou ao.

join our world.

Victor Billot

Lost in Space

Estuarine sand sucks at wet boots.
Bubbles and the creep of small life.
The galaxy turns above,
the close air muted, easy.
Reef and clusters frozen beyond time.
You stand and watch in shadow.
After everything, we still share this.
The galaxy turns on. Salt and humid earth.
All held in the hands of night.
We are outside ourselves.
Beyond redemption.
Yet the brutal year steps away.
Something must be returned.
This is what it was like, sometimes.
The cruellest suggestion of hope.
Is there hope? None.
The wine red on our lips
and sour. I remember this.
The struggle in the waves,
the drowning struggle.
The galaxy turns
and this is the last of our time.
There is no returning.
Even as we step carefully back
in silence, I am walking away,
under the wheel of stars.

Wes Lee

Wearing the Night
After Joanne Burns's 'Keyhole'

i. machinery

Wearing the night like a lifesaving dummy.
kneeling before your open mouth. an abandoned
mall. copper pipe. hidden architecture: wires
hanging from the ceiling like stalactites. this new
world where things close and never open again.
the architecture of your email. a sharpened
shell. like an omission. like your steady gaze.
a fragile core. a pyramid scheme. *your hand*
never reached for the first rung; you never wanted to climb
the crazy Seussian tower of topple. doors designed
to be visible only to those who are trained to see.
and the rest, we hammer and wonder and cry. wearing
the night like the grim northern gums of your ancestors.
cancer sticks set out on trays at half time. the matinee
of eyes. in the room where hearts are discussed
swims the ghost of your mother's death. a plastic
model of a life-size heart. the new world has come quickly:
automatic, cash free, desolate. like the captured
eye of the swift, unfocused on our reality. *and I*
remembered how you said you were happy that the nurses
liked your mother for her sense of humour. and we would
be two humans in a room where anything could
happen. and the nurse said can you relax
your legs, just allow them to flop. wearing the night
like money to keep us safe from pain, feeding it
in our clothes, slotted over our hearts. *'we can*
still leave the building,' I told you: the wide balustrade
opening out to a glass door, to the hospital carpark where
we could drive. like lush machinery. like 3am:

the miraculous moment when the fibrillation
stopped; the heart quietened. one moment then
another changed moment. tensed on the bed, driven
crazy by maracas out of sync. *the clean miracle*
his body made. wearing the night like indelible words.
hitting the truth hard. like deciding you are
the galleon and you could co-exist in the tank
with the fish. sink quietly to the bottom. two
did not make it out of childhood, one dead at birth;
quietly as he came from them, almost slipped in.
and I thought about a few of the nurses, later, in the day's
drift, in the dream I needed. and I kept whispering
each time the animal struggled in my chest: stay in the
dream, the living waking dream. dropping each arising
thought that did not fit with the dream, that did not talk
to the dream.

ii. firefly

Wearing the night like keeping company with fire.
a snake takes the night into its body, dislocating
its jaw. a sheet in the forest canopy collects insects.
I write — it's how I judge myself and feel better. if I stopped,
what would I do?[1] wearing the night like a child pulled
in a carriage by a pig, rushing along a dark midnight
road with the moon above, shrieking with joy, and
the pig so obviously happy. like Larkin using the
moon to say things about youth and aging. *to know*
this comfort is but a station. a man chasing that moment
he cannot stop chasing: that crack of bone where

---

1   *I write — it's how I judge myself and feel better. If I stopped, what would I*
    do? paraphrases a quote from Jon Ronson on Randy Newman in Kate Leaver,
    'The VICE interview: Jon Ronson', *Vice*, 4 October 2016, https://vice.com/en/
    article/9b8kvy/the-vice-interview-jon-ronson

object meets human; like having your lights punched
out. all the world's praise with words like *peerless* and
delighted and *thrilling*, pushing you further and further
away from yourself, banging the tin of disappointment
and worthlessness, bringing up the spectre of future
homelessness, poverty and sickness and all that befalls.
wearing the night like doing what is manageable.
waiting for something to tug at your coat. a lake
of silence. filling your gaze with the stable horizon.
the evidence of poetry. the world in each breath.
the sheet collects hoping to find something new:
a firefly, as yet unseen. a surge of hands. a fan wafted
over memory. merciless. it burns.

iii. eternal

Wearing the night like the static you have heard all your life
    suddenly drops. a nurse holding the phone
    up to your father's mask, trying to catch the last
    seconds of his life. the smallness of the type
    in a poetry book. smoke that seems to say
    there was a fire. a sharp intake of breath. a girding
    of the heart. *at fifteen, Kerry, at twenty-three, Fiona,*
    who died because of their hearts. wearing the night
    like a newborn clutching an IUD; an apocryphal tale.
    the realisation that wakes you: *I have never really*
    told the story of my life. like a hand sliding under
    a white towel. redemption skitters away, the obligatory
    happy ending. sluggishly waking. *as if we have all*
    been sleeping. the eternal sun of a California funeral.

iv. help

Wearing the night like the detective who cried
    when he spoke of finding the missing child:
    I had newspapers tell me: We've done our paedophile
    story this year — people don't want to know — our readers,
    they're happy with the Lolita image of an older girl
    but when it comes to one- and three- and five-year-olds
    they don't want their minds to go there.[2] and that night
    you made a sound; unintelligible to your ears.
    the sound you knew later when you realised
    you were calling, what you were trying to shout.

---

2 'iv. help' paraphrases information from Chris Smith, *The Disappearance of Madeleine McCann*, California: Paramount Television Studios, 2019.

Obliterated Affairs

Pouring drinks like you were on death row,
you hyped the party
like a tequila bass drop.
Your face-splitting grin seared her chest.
When you ushered firelit lies
along her collarbone in the moonless night.

At midnights
she is awake as an endless nothing.
Uninvited messages arouse her screen.
Self-respect creaks out the door
when she lets
your sheepskin-lined leather coat
come in her again.

Daisy heads bow to their befallen on the sill.
Once you scrambled eggs
laden with butter,
dripping fresh cream.
Now sour dregs of the coffee grind
lace her lonely tongue.

A dish stack wallows beside the sink.
She draws a finger through the dust,
steadily your name appears.

You erase with a swipe of her hand.

a crack lets in the darkness, too

Today
I knock a glass into the kitchen sink while
doing dishes the glass ricochets twice against
the unforgiving ceramic plinks etching
themselves into the wincing lines of my face
I make a billion tiny deals with the universe in
the breath between bounces a crack spreads
up one side of the glass it holds it holds it holds
it collapses into jagged pieces have you seen
that one channel on TikTok where she creates
dances from videos of objects being crushed
I am a sheaf of paper a handful of gummy bears
an old analogue alarm clock I spill out the sides
of myself in clumps and spikes and a hundred
tiny jagged pieces hours later I gather up the
shards ungloved watch swirls of red tidy
themselves away down the drain

Yesterday
you spilled out of yourself in grainy black gushes
while I held your hand and a bucket I wanted to
find a way to put your pieces back together kintsugi-
style but you were beyond the desire to mend I
held I held I held I let go and you went a little
quiet and a little rage nothing but a crumpled cup
completely empty people aren't
supposed to have corners

I wrap the shards in newspaper dull the sharp
edges bleeding is only allowed in small private
doses

Essays

Beneath the Linden Trees: Richard von Sturmer and the Mind of Meditation

And if anyone were to ask me what this practice is — this practice of
Zen — I would have to say:

It's simply the pleasure
of watching patches of sunlight and shadows
glide over the coat of an old man
as he walks beneath the linden trees.[1]

Richard von Sturmer's poetry might first appear to exemplify the
kind of quirky, quotidian realism for which Williams Carlos Williams
is so famously remembered. Written in a mode that could be
characterised as descriptive-objective, his poetry shares many aesthetic
characteristics with the twentieth-century imagists. The plums, the
icebox; the sunlight, the linden trees; the emphasis on seeing minute
particulars clearly. What might be less clear is the way that his writing
is underpinned by a rigorous form of psychosomatic practice in the
tradition of Zen Buddhism.

As both a formal student of Buddhism and an accomplished writer,
Richard von Sturmer holds a singular place in the artistic landscape
of Aotearoa New Zealand. For over a decade, he and his wife, Amala
Wrightson, lived and worked at a residential Zen training centre in
upstate New York, where they studied a demanding curriculum of
meditation as well as the liturgical and literary canons of the Zen
tradition.[2] Many of von Sturmer's subsequent books situate themselves
in dialogue with Zen Buddhist literature, from the kōan collections of
medieval Japan and China to contemporary western Zen writing. His
poetry is often structured as a response to existing Buddhist literature,
creating a transhistorical, transcultural, intertextual conversation.[3] The
dominant aesthetic characteristics of his poetry arise as a reflection
of his meditation practice, and invoke a centuries-old tradition as he
aspires to yoke ontological and poetic experience.

Richard von Sturmer's writing arises as an unself-conscious manifestation of his being in the world. Contrary to the modernist notion of art as artifice, von Sturmer's poetry is an embodied way of regarding his surrounds, cultivated through intensive training in meditation. The seemingly effortless realism of his Zen poetry actually requires, as Allen Ginsberg once observed, 'a life's preparation in practicing awareness ... to stay in the body and observe the space around [one]'.[4]

Put differently, von Sturmer's most characteristic style markers arise from his meditation practice. While other poets may practise as a way of dealing with emotional confusions or a means of 'self-expression', von Sturmer's Zen-influenced poetry empties out a sense of self. His poetry has a measured and factual tone, suggesting an absence of striving and a tendency towards impersonal or 'objective' modes of description. As such, most of von Sturmer's writing demonstrates a kind of emotional stability — a calmness, an unruffled place from which to be open and receptive. His writing is marked by an attentiveness to the phenomenal world which Zen meditation practitioners seek to develop, and many of the adjectives one might use to describe von Sturmer's poetry are the same qualities sought in Zen meditation: unobtrusive, observant, calm, detached, composed.

In the history of Zen Buddhist literature, the possibility of one's meditation practice informing one's poetic practice is a recurring point of contemplation for poets and scholars: Su Shih (1037–1101), a Ch'an[5] poet and statesman of the Sung Dynasty, insisted that one's consciousness must first be characterised by emptiness and quietude if one is to produce worthwhile poetry.[6] T'ang Dynasty poet and critic Liu Yü-hsi (772–842) theorised an ideal state 'in which the interdependent functions of perception and verbal articulation attain perfect and natural spontaneity'.[7]

In this ideal marriage of meditation and poetry, poetry would arise at the moment of perception itself as an embodied act of apprehending the world. Meditation practice would be an experiential methodology for the composition of poetry, and bring about a psychosomatic state in which 'ontological and poetic experience are one'.[8]

rollerblades and sparrows
cut straight through
the late afternoon sunlight[9]

Von Sturmer's poetic practice also reflects ideas expounded by recent
figures in the Zen tradition such as twentieth-century teacher Shunryu
Suzuki. In his book *Zen Mind, Beginner's Mind*,[10] Suzuki explains that
a practitioner should aspire to maintain a meditative state of mind
in all activities, and that any activity, when done with single-minded
concentration, is as good as zazen:[11]

> To cook, or to fix some food, is not preparation, according to Dōgen;
> it is practice . . . You should work on it with nothing in your mind,
> and without expecting anything. You should just cook! That is also an
> experience of our sincerity, a part of our practice . . . Whatever you do, it
> should be an expression of the same deep activity [as zazen].[12]

As von Sturmer himself says, one of the purposes of undertaking Zen
training is so that one can 'integrate the clarity and concentration
of the zendo[13] into everyday life', so that one's practice 'becomes a
moving zazen, a zazen that expresses itself through our actions and
interactions'.[14]

Since enlightenment is 'an awakening to a pre-existing reality
rather than an accomplishment to be achieved',[15] maintaining a
meditative state of mind in all one's activities — including writing —
is not something to be worked towards as much as something to be
remembered. The meditative state of mind, according to Suzuki, should
be devoid of any thoughts of starting points, goals or attainment.[16] As
such, zazen is a 'practice free from gaining ideas',[17] an activity in which
there should be no striving.

The founder of Sōtō Zen, Eihei Dōgen (1200–1253), emphasised that
any conscious endeavour in zazen is illusory: 'Zazen is not thinking of
good, nor thinking of bad. It is not conscious endeavor.'[18] It requires a
kind of 'effortless effort', a middle way between action and inaction, an

unforced action which appears as if spontaneously manifesting rather than as the result of conscious action on the part of the meditator.[19]

In fact, particular types of Zen meditation, including zazen, are described as a mode of consciousness characterised by 'non-thinking'.[20] As one allows all discriminative thoughts to dissipate, the mind becomes empty. Introspection and speculation are relinquished in favour of a not-knowing, a non-thinking, an emptying-out. For American Zen poet Jane Hirshfield, this particular kind of non-thinking, not-knowing concentration is common to both poetry and meditation: a state in which 'the mind [is] open, inclusive, alert, receptive to whatever comes, quietly aware'.[21]

The open and empty mind becomes, as Hirshfield suggests, ready to be filled with whatever enters it. For earlier Ch'an poets, too, 'receptivity is the key point': 'being ready and able to resonate with what reveals itself'.[22] T'ang poet Liu Yü-hsi confirms this when he says that keeping a mind clear of thoughts and desires is what allows the 'myriad forms of phenomenal reality' to enter it.[23] For his part, von Sturmer describes Zen training as a kind of emptying out of the mind and self: 'If you allow yourself to become empty, then the world can reveal itself to you in a sparkling way.'[24] All of these writers in the Zen tradition suggest that poetic composition first demands an empty mind. As a common Buddhist metaphor figures it, one should make the mind a mirror for the phenomenal world.

Following Suzuki's explanation of meditation as a 'practice free from gaining ideas' and a 'single-minded way',[25] the speaker of von Sturmer's poetry says that to notice a fallen leaf is enough to keep him on the right track:

When I return to Auckland in a few weeks, things will not be so simple. But the city has its own continuity: buses will stop for passengers at bus stops; mail keeps on being delivered; food appears on the shelves of supermarkets. In spring, fireworks will briefly light up the night sky; by summer the smell of mildew will have begun to rise from the piles of old books in the secondhand bookshop at the end of the arcade; and on the balcony of a restored villa, an Alsatian dog will poke his head between the balustrades, as he did the year before, and bark frenetically as I walk past. This is sufficient; I will take the barking to be a confirmation. And afterwards, to see a sparrow or a fallen leaf will also be enough to keep me on the right track.[26]

The importance of the speaker in the above paragraph is downplayed, his role being merely the observer of small birds or inconstant sounds. Instead, objects and animals[27] are given a degree of agency. The city, the sum of all movement, has its own particular rhythm formed by the agency of objects, machines and animals; buses, fireworks, food, dogs, sparrows and falling leaves all mobilise themselves. The degree of agency afforded to objects and animals is reflective of the non-attachment that is cultivated in zazen: allowing thoughts to pass through the mind without needing to accept, reject or control them, a process described by Jane Hirshfield:

> If you are in shikantaza,[28] and do[ing] shikantaza, [and] a thought comes: it's just like any other phenomenon. The ideal would be the image of a lake and a cloud that goes through the sky. The lake does not grasp the cloud and it does not accept the reflection on its surface. If there is a cloud, there is a cloud. The lake does not care. The lake is just being a lake.[29]

Here, Hirshfield connects the process of watching thoughts with the practice of allowing other beings to move about unhindered by human attachment. This sense of detachment and non-controlling on the part of the meditator allows other non-human beings to have agency and autonomy, in life as well as in poetry.

As well as being filled with the movements and sounds of objects and animals, von Sturmer's poetry seems also to actually be motivated by objects and animals. Rather than having any internal impetus to write for the sake of externalising his thoughts, von Sturmer's writing seems to be dependent on and driven by his environment. In 'Barrier Crossings', and later in 'The Bodhisattvic Garden', the natural environment dictates the shape of the writing:

a green haze
deep in the valley,
when I finish my paragraph
the wind tells me
it's time to turn the page[30]

Today, having nothing to write down, I leave my notebook open on
one of the tables. As the pages flutter in a light breeze, the white paper
with its thin blue lines absorbs the chattering of nearby sparrows, the
scuttling of a squirrel as it spirals down a tree trunk, the flickering of
someone walking briskly behind a fence.[31]

In allowing the distinction between the personal (the psychological
concerns of the poet) and the impersonal (the wind, the sparrows,
the squirrel) to fall away, these verses aspire to a kind of non-duality
between mind and environment. Both the writing practice and the
meditation practice aim towards an expansion of the boundaries of the
self until it encompasses everything, so that there is no person inside
'here' and no external world 'out there'.[32] Although von Sturmer's
first collection of Zen-focused writing, *Suchness: Zen Poetry and
Prose*, is framed as an autobiographical set of writings, it is also full of
impersonal and seemingly objective observations in which the private
feelings of the individual psyche are omitted.

It could be said that what von Sturmer aspires towards in poetry
and in meditation is an ontological cancellation of *thinking about* the
(separate) world, and a *non-thinking communion with* the phenomenal
world. Certainly, what attracts me to von Sturmer's poetry is that it offers
a path for the reader to do the same. For one who is interested in the
soteriological functions of writing (that is to say, how religious literatures
attempt to lead their readers towards salvation), von Sturmer's poetry
offers ample encouragement. His practice of bringing mundane settings
into the sphere of meditative inquiry is an embodied understanding of
Buddhist teachings, including *anātman* (no-self), *anitya* (impermanence)
and an enhanced sense of intimacy with all beings.

Perhaps most appealing about von Sturmer's poetic practice, and the tradition of Zen poetry in general, is that its approach to religious learning doesn't require familiarisation with a corpus of specialised vocabulary and esoteric doctrines. Instead, the tradition consciously strives to be indistinguishable from — or at least, sit close to — the secular literatures of its times.[33] When enthusiasts and novices appear with complex philosophical questions about the 'true nature of things', they are directed away from intellectual abstractions and toward a meditative communion with the phenomenal world. Through demonstration, Zen literature enacts a referential pointing that invites the reader to notice the phenomena in their own environment.

Kōan[34] case 37 from *The Gateless Gate* stages this dynamic when a monk asks why Bodhidharma, the founding figure of Zen, travelled northeast from India to expound Buddhist teachings:

A monk asked Jōshū [Chao-chou][35] why Bodhidharma came to China. Jōshū said: 'An oak tree in the garden.'[36]

Jōshū's deictic statement[37] encourages the monk to relinquish myriad thoughts about the meaning of Zen, and the indirection between the question and the answer implicitly suggests the futility of trying to understand experiential truths through logical reasoning. In a similar way, von Sturmer takes abstract concepts of Buddhism and turns them into referential statements with concrete nouns and active verbs, implicitly suggesting that the curious reader would do best to turn a meditative attention to their own surrounds.

And if anyone were to ask me what this practice is — this practice of Zen — I would have to say:

It's simply the pleasure
of watching patches of sunlight and shadows
glide over the coat of an old man
as he walks beneath the linden trees.[38]

1 Richard von Sturmer, 'Time and Light'. In *Suchness: Zen Poetry and Prose* (Wellington: Headworx, 2005), 147–48.

2 Their practice and study of Zen continued in a new form from the early 2000s, when the couple moved back to Tāmaki Makaurau and founded the Auckland Zen Centre.

3 See, for example, the *Book of Equanimity Verses* (Auckland: Puriri Press, 2013), a collection of 100 poems that correlate to the 100 kōan cases in the thirteenth-century Chinese *Book of Equanimity: Illuminating classic Zen koans*; and *Suchness*, which consists of poems that respond to Buddhist concepts, practices and kōans. Richard von Sturmer's Zen-influenced poetry generally makes extensive use of forms traditional to Japanese literature (*tanka*, haiku, *haibun*, *zuihitsu*), such as in *Resonating Distances* (Pokeno: Titus Books, 2022). Although each of his poetic responses are intended to function discretely as self-contained texts, meaning that they can be read by those who are unfamiliar with Buddhist ideas, practices or literature, when read in combination with earlier Buddhist texts, they enact a dialogue and compound points of view on the same inquiry or topic.

4 Quoted in Kent Johnson and Craig Paulenich, eds., *Beneath a Single Moon: Buddhism in Contemporary American Poetry* (Boston, MA: Shambhala, 1991), 97.

5 'Zen' is the Japanese name for a particular school of Mahāyāna Buddhism which originated in China in the sixth century CE and was established in Japan in the twelfth century. While using the term 'Zen' to refer to the school in general, I use its Chinese name, 'Ch'an', when speaking specifically about a Chinese context. I've used Wade–Giles romanisation for Chinese words and names in keeping with the majority of the scholarship I have consulted.

6 Richard John Lynn, 'The Sudden and the Gradual in Chinese Poetry Criticism: An Examination of the Ch'an-Poetry Analogy', in Peter N. Gregory, ed., *Sudden and Gradual: Approaches to Enlightenment in Chinese Thought* (Delhi: Motilal Banarsidass Publishers, 1991), 385.

7 Lynn, 'The Sudden and the Gradual', 384.

8 Chung-yuan Chang, *Creativity and Taoism: A Study of Chinese Philosophy, Art and Poetry* (New York, NY: Harper and Row, 1970), 174.

9 Von Sturmer, 'Sparrow Notebook (1995/1996)', *Suchness*, 40.

10 One of the most well-known and bestselling books on Zen meditation in English.

11 Seated meditation, a 'non-thinking mode of consciousness'. Carl Olson and Charles S. Prebish, *The A to Z of Buddhism* (Lanham, MD: Scarecrow Press, 2009), 245.

12 Shunryu Suzuki, *Zen Mind, Beginner's Mind: Informal Talks on Zen Meditation and Practice* (New York, NY/Tokyo: Weatherhill, 1995), 37–38.

13 The meditation hall at a Zen monastery or centre.

14 Richard von Sturmer and Joseph Sorrentino, *Images from the Center: Daily Life at an American Zen Center* (Rochester, NY: Rochester Zen Center, 1998), 9.

15 Sandra Wawrytko, 'The Poetics of Ch'an: Upayic Poetry and Its Taoist Enrichment', *Chung-Hwa Buddhist Journal* 5 (1992): 373.

16 Suzuki, *Zen Mind*, 38.

17 Ibid., 25.

18 Kazuaki Tanahashi, ed. *Treasury of the True Dharma Eye: Zen Master Dōgen's Shobo Genzo* (Boston, MA: Shambhala, 2011), 29.

19 J. P. Williams, *Denying Divinity: Apophasis in the Patristic Christian and Soto Zen Buddhist Traditions* (Oxford: Oxford University Press, 2000), 50. Williams notes that this conception of 'effortless effort' in Zen owes a great debt to the Taoist concept of *wu-wei*, 'actionless action'.

20 Williams, *Denying Divinity*, 49; Olson and Prebish, *The A to Z of Buddhism*, 245.

21 Jane Hirshfield, 'Poetry, Zazen and the Net of Connection', in *Beneath a Single Moon: Buddhism in Contemporary American Poetry*, ed. Kent Johnson and Craig Paulenich (Boston, MA: Shambhala, 1991), 150.

22 Wawrytko, 'The Poetics of Ch'an', 353.

23 Lynn, 'The Sudden and the Gradual', 384.

24 Gabriel White, 'Both Sides of the Street', in *Rubble Emits Light* (Auckland: The Film Archive, 2009), 8.

25 Suzuki, *Zen Mind*, 25, 53.

26 Von Sturmer, 'Writing with Issa', *Suchness*, 139–40.

27 'Objects and animals' is an unsatisfactory way of referring to the diverse sentient and insentient beings that fill von Sturmer's poetry. However, as I am trying to emphasise the vividness and physicality of 'things' in this context, I think the grouping 'objects and animals' works better than more ambiguous terms like 'phenomena' or 'environment'.

28 Referred to as 'just sitting', a Zen meditation technique developed by Sōtō school founder Dōgen (1200–1253).

29 Chung Ling, 'Jane Hirshfield's Poetic Voice and Zen Meditation', in *American Modernist Poetry and the Chinese Encounter*, ed. Zhang Yuejun and Stuart Christie (New York, NY: Palgrave Macmillan, 2012), 158–59.

30 Von Sturmer, 'Barrier Crossings', *Suchness*, 99.

31 Von Sturmer, 'The Bodhisattvic Garden', *Suchness*, 149.

32 Suzuki, *Zen Mind*, 44.

33 Burton Watson, 'Zen Poetry', in *Zen: Tradition and Transition: A Sourcebook by Contemporary Zen Masters and Scholars*, ed. Kenneth Kraft (New York, NY: Grove Press, 1988), 106–7.

34 Kōans, which have their roots in T'ang dynasty China (618–907) (called 'kung-an' in Chinese contexts), are a literary form peculiar to Zen. Functioning as a kind of puzzle, they are regarded alternately as vehicles to spiritual achievement and highly stylised literary texts. Usually structured as an enigmatic dialogue between a Zen master and student or a cryptic narrative, kōans feature minimal verbiage, indirection, and the impulse toward full silence.

35 Chao-chou Ts'ung-shen (778–897) was a Ch'an master famous for his paradoxical statements and strange gestures. In Nyogen Senzaki and Paul Reps' translation of *The Gateless Gate*, his name is rendered in the Japanese transliteration 'Jōshū'.

36 Paul Reps, ed. *Zen Flesh, Zen Bones* (Middlesex/Melbourne: Pelican Books, 1973), 123.

37 In other translations, the deictic mode is more clearly expressed. For example, Jōshū's reply is sometimes figured as 'the oak tree there in the garden', or 'the cypress tree there in the courtyard'.

38 Von Sturmer, 'Time and Light', *Suchness*, 147–48.

Works Cited

Chang, Chung-yuan. *Creativity and Taoism: A Study of Chinese Philosophy, Art and Poetry*. New York, NY: Harper and Row, 1970.

Hirshfield, Jane. 'Poetry, Zazen and the Net of Connection.' In *Beneath a Single Moon: Buddhism in Contemporary American Poetry*, edited by Kent Johnson and Craig Paulenich, 149–53. Boston, MA: Shambhala, 1991.

Johnson, Kent, and Craig Paulenich, eds. *Beneath a Single Moon: Buddhism in Contemporary American Poetry*. Boston, MA: Shambhala, 1991.

Ling, Chung. 'Jane Hirshfield's Poetic Voice and Zen Meditation.' In *American Modernist Poetry and the Chinese Encounter*, edited by Zhang Yuejun and Stuart Christie, 153–78. New York, NY: Palgrave Macmillan, 2012.

Lynn, Richard John. 'The Sudden and the Gradual in Chinese Poetry Criticism: An Examination of the Ch'an-Poetry Analogy.' In *Sudden and Gradual: Approaches to Enlightenment in Chinese Thought*, edited by Peter N. Gregory, 381–428. Delhi: Motilal Banarsidass Publishers, 1991.

Olson, Carl, and Charles S. Prebish. *The A to Z of Buddhism*. Lanham, MD: Scarecrow Press, 2009.

Reps, Paul, ed. *Zen Flesh, Zen Bones*. Middlesex/ Melbourne: Pelican Books, 1973.

Suzuki, Shunryu. *Zen Mind, Beginner's Mind: Informal Talks on Zen Meditation and Practice*. New York, NY/Tokyo: Weatherhill, 1995.

Tanahashi, Kazuaki, ed. *Treasury of the True Dharma Eye: Zen Master Dōgen's Shobo Genzo*. Boston, MA: Shambhala, 2011.

Von Sturmer, Richard. *Book of Equanimity Verses*. Auckland: Puriri Press, 2013.

Resonating Distances. Pokeno: Titus Books, 2022.

Suchness: Zen Poetry and Prose. Wellington: HeadworX, 2005.

Von Sturmer, Richard, and Joseph Sorrentino. *Images from the Center: Daily Life at an American Zen Center*. Rochester, NY: Rochester Zen Center, 1998.

Watson, Burton. 'Zen Poetry.' In *Zen: Tradition and Transition: A Sourcebook by Contemporary Zen Masters and Scholars*, edited by Kenneth Kraft, 105–24. New York, NY: Grove Press, 1988.

Wawrytko, Sandra. 'The Poetics of Ch'an: Upayic Poetry and Its Taoist Enrichment.' *Chung-Hwa Buddhist Journal* 5 (1992): 341–78.

White, Gabriel. 'Both Sides of the Street.' In *Rubble Emits Light*, 1–13. Auckland: The Film Archive, 2009.

Williams, J. P. *Denying Divinity: Apophasis in the Patristic Christian and Soto Zen Buddhist Traditions*. Oxford: Oxford University Press, 2000.

John Geraets

Constant Structure
What is wrong with the expectations we place on language?

There are innumerable centres and positions for us to occupy.[1]

*

The contemporary non-realist philosopher Hilary Lawson insists that the act of 'closure' is unavoidable and characterises our ways of 'holding' the world as supposed reality. Closure is an act of selective definition made in the face of an openness that eludes final containment. Our acts of art — our actions as humans, period — are forms of illusion or misrepresentation.[2] We hold the world in certain ways according to our needs and in order to make *proper* use of it — in the end, Lawson tells us, reality is 'unholdable'.[3]

*

This writing claims no home or way there; nonetheless, it will state preferences with candour. Poetry performs repeated incursions — call them *self-incisions* — into the corpus of language that elicit accounts of experiential occupancy in the world. Consider Charles Brasch's heartfelt plea in 'The Silent Land':

> Man must lie with the gaunt hills like a lover,
> Earning their intimacy in the calm sigh

or Ursula Bethell's intense act of supplication in 'Time':

> Oh, become established quickly, quickly, garden
> For I am fugitive

or Allen Curnow's quashing of distance into the waning 'eye of day' at Karekare beach in 'Lone Kauri Road':

The first time I looked seaward, westward,
it was looking back yellowly,
a dulling incandescence.

Simply put, there's no definitive answer to be found in poetic texts or elsewhere. As we enter the new land of artificial intelligence (AI), we look back and see that our habitual ways of writing and reading have been helplessly self-centred, anthropomorphic.[4] Our local history of poetry channels the world of sensory input into an assemblage of intersubjectivity. We have made the world a feature of an interposed, all-encompassing, capital letter *first* person 'I'. We have sought to outreckon God.

*

This piece of writing — a matter of floating shards — defenestrates the subject-making that has long underpinned the 'held' in poetry. Such subjectivity is implicated in an implacable conjuring up, projecting and subjugating of the discoverable world in an extenuation of self or selves. Or, to put it another way: I attest a poetics of bottomless infinitude. Firm footing in the world is an oxymoron in the order of futility. This involves more than fatal attraction.

*

John Coltrane's rendition of 'My Favourite Things' evokes — yet is clearly not identical to — the instantly recognisable original tune. When Albert Ayler performs 'Spiritual Unity', he shatters God and the world into a thousand fragments. Timing and timbre in music are everything to play for, with. *Originality* is the lure. Thus, it comes to language and poetry. There is, in poet Ann Lauterbach's phrase, only the *given* and the *chosen* of attention.[5] Yet distinctions are to be made.

*

Like the reflexive 'I' on which it is posited, poetic language affirms an innerness that evades final encounter, try as one might. No *essence* lurks. The language cannot help but fall between the two because, like chicanery or a form of fiat currency, it is granted (nowadays precarious!) value without rock-solid foundations. A thing is something, although never a self-sufficient anything; it invites its opposite, and is what it is by virtue of what it's not. And even *that* sentence prevaricates.

There is inevitable proliferation, papañca (Sanskrit: prapañca) as the Buddha terms it. Sages point a finger to the moon (who points nowhere?) — presumably to alert us to the limits of looking and knowing: 'The description is not the final thing. And yet it is not pointless', remarks Donald Hoffman.[6] The pun, admittedly, is mine: every*thing*, every word, iterates contingency, a makeshift placing within an assumed or fabricated assemblage. Kendrick Smithyman is the local poet who has explored such terrain most assiduously:

A yellow-breasted bird
heraldic upon a rock
devised himself to give back
due light to the afternoon.
Who from his posing took
strength, as from the sun.
('Kingfisher Song', my italics)

The 'who' is 'himself', a proximate 'I', reflexively male. Smithyman recognises that pronouns are implicit claims upon the material presented. In loosening their hold, he incidentally tosses settled ownership to the wind. Furthermore, 'heraldic' might as well apply to the above lines quoted from Curnow, whereby time and distance collapse in an emblazoned gazing into an abyss — something an earlier poem refers to as 'To sink both self and all why sink the whole / Phenomenal enterprise' ('To Forget Self and All'). Subjectivity does get pretty weird.

Smithyman's later work engages more explicitly in such 'Deconstructing':

I'm not going to try describing that run
from down by the creek where it starts being
a river, up to the ridge where everything falls
away westward. For the first time again
you look out on a sea bigger, further, than remembered.

Assuredly, there is a (befuddled) 'I' leading the way; however,
the playfulness — here as elsewhere — has less to do with self-
declaration and more with a realisation that efforts at self-existence are
perspectival, improvised. Conveniently, the speaker transmutes into
'you'. It is within reality's non-existent *ur*-house that poetry prepares a
dwelling.[7] Smithyman I consider to be our pre-eminent non-realist poet.

*

The word 'culprit' is not what it implies.
Neither derives from the other, nor does
either give rise to this incarnation. That's
what free agents are. It is designated the
entire language of our insouciance. Whether
a queen or a ruffled flower, culprit baulks.

*

Transitions in poetic centres in Aotearoa New Zealand intrigue me.[8]
In the early twentieth century, male poets were considered the serious
thinkers and women largely poetasters. The subsequent revolutions
of the thirties, seventies and eighties, and the noughties reveal an
interesting set of progressions, not only of poetics in relation to the
world, but also the way in which 'I' is refigured. From the late sixties
onward, youthful, activist, female and Māori voices have become
increasingly unashamed, outspoken, activist. In the present century,
the rapid evolution into multi-gendered, multi-ethnic and multi-
poetic viewpoints has been remarkable to behold, as witnessed in the

appearance of the whopping queer anthology *Out Here*.[9]

In all these eras, what were our poets thinking? What are we to make of their shaping th*our* world? On whose behalf? And how to encompass such expansive accommodations with precision? Like the Matisse of the late cut-outs, where the shapes rendered are not reducible to a beforehand or straightforward extrapolation of importance, shaping-sounding-scripting have their own meaning. And articulating (an articulation of) the shaping is still another shaping. Meaning endlessly extrapolates. There are innumerable centres and positions to adopt: a poem means giving shape. The one it *is* as much as those it is *not*.

*

What does Joanna Paul evoke when she paints an image or writes a poem about the interior of a house or a body? Is this contrary to the Brasch–Curnow possession of the world? Look at this account of habitation of interspersed spaces, I-not-I, signalling disarray in the location of identity.[10]

Here Paul places the misalignment between assumption and encounter into prominent question. It is not that an answer to the question is sought, much less assumed; rather, the questioning takes the form of slivers of incompleteness within a squeezed disclosure. Such exploration I see occurring in diverse ways in the work of Anna Jackson (psychoaesthics), Michele Leggott (mythopoetics), Richard von Sturmer (zenaesthics), Robert Sullivan (ethnoaesthics), essa may ranapiri (gendaesthics), Emma Barnes and Chris Tse (queeraesthics), Iain Britton (ecoaesthics) and Lisa Samuels (aesaesthics), among others. The father/progenitor of such proliferation in poetic mode — wittingly or unwittingly, given his own insouciance — I take to be Mark Young (aesthetics).

A question that has yet to be properly addressed is: is form proprietary? And what happens when we are given too much of a good thing, too many things?[11] Are we — our poetry — our splaying human predilections — in an unfortunate state of surfeit?

*

We hug subjectivity like a rock. 'I' isn't happening inside *my* body.

The course of 'human civilisation' does not prevail.

This contra: 'Yuval Noah Harari argues that AI has hacked the operating system of human civilisation'.[12]

Whence the anti-intellectualism of the flamboyant 'I'?

Well-thought-out positions haven't yet managed to save the world. Nor poorly thought-out ones. The hyphen is the culprit.

To reject art on any other basis than form is legitimate, while at the same time it is a desecration of art. Only art is content with the contradiction.

Reality (abhors) stasis. Nor is it still or moving.

*

Poetry is non-definitive. It registers hard points along a referential path (which it endeavours to respect), in the process finding that what holds constant is constantly breaking down. Poetry is witness to the entropy of human endeavour. Alone (with other art forms) it's an intimation that cannot be finally intimated: the extenuation of prospect, ad libitum:

> The way Bill's blue hydrangeas open in the
> air, occupying it. For me, when I open, I am
> aware of a certain resistance, *theirs* and
> mine.

As content collapses, or dissipates over time, it reverts to form. What belongs to poetry — and what doesn't? Things are the way they are held.

> This happens near Bill's place, where
> various hydrangeas pop among leaves like
> oversized blue bulbs. When I see them, I am
> reminded of Annette, who regularly attends
> the Zen steps, and is nothing like either Bill
> or the bulbs or shielding hedges, or the
> flattened leaves, though she cleans the steps.
> *Where angels cautiously tread.*

*

Out Here is an extraordinary book of uber-claim on the power of the pronoun, especially in relation to the exercise of gender and sexual orientation in contemporary society.[13] But for all the upheaval of traditional pronoun use — ranapiri turnstiles 'i, xe, xir, their, ur' — the singular 'I' proves the hardest to shake off. One way or another, everyone remains resolutely attached to self-authentication. When I speak, I wrap myself thus: 'I'. But what is an 'I', and who is one?

Within strange promise and translucency — like a sky rocket propelled upward only to suddenly expire in a brilliant array of multicoloured individual lights — I read with interest the steady launch of new poetry sites and book publications (in a sampling from the New Zealand poetry rack at the Takapuna library in Auckland): Oscar Upperton's *New Transgender Blockbusters* (2020), Jordan Hamel's *Everyone is everyone except you* (2022), Vana Manasiadis's *The Grief Almanac: A Sequel* (2019), Lynley Edmeades's *Listening In* (2019), Emma Barnes's *I am in Bed with You* (2020), Jake Arthur's *A Lack of Good Sons* (2023). These are fresh, exhilarating sky-shots. If I express a reservation, it concerns their narrowed orbits round the moon of subjectivity. Let me illustrate, not unkindly, with two and a half lines taken from Barnes's *I am in Bed with You*:

> I capital I capital I start these sentences in my
> head on the night I have an existential crisis
> about my gender
> ('I am a man')

Six self-references, plus one in the title. The unaddressed crisis nestled within the highlighted gender crisis, deserving as it is of attention, is our settled, untroubled adoption of 'I' as the 'true' source of authority to speak and choose and need.

We risk reverting to form as content's support, like a coat hanger on which a garment is arrayed. There is nothing wrong with using form to convey content, or treasuring poetry based on content. On the other hand, the argument presented here is that it is form that makes content possible and not the other way around. It's form we must somehow crack.

*

Nestled in the opening pages of *Out Here* is slightly older queer poet Alison Glenny.[14] But 'queer' here intimates the earlier sense of an unusualness that eludes definition. Her *Bird Collector* is a poetics of antithesis, metamorphosis, anywhere everywhere and vice versa. It opens:

'But we do not know in advance *which* key will unlock the hidden melody. Discovering it is a matter of chance — like opening a drawer at random and finding snow, or the ghost of a bird fluttering among the cogs and feathers'. The composer fell silent, leaving Odile to ponder his gift; the way it grew heavier the closer she approached. Eventually she would have to unwrap the box, burn the finely embossed paper. There was no telling what they might glimpse among the ashes. The remains of field notes or the charred pages of a poem — its ruined homologies. A book of instructions on how to mourn, which gradations of ribbons and ornaments. She sensed that the question would continue to revolve as they turned the handle, a machine releasing oracles that were mistaken for songs.
('Key')

Encapsulated in this beautiful paragraph is much of what I wish to say. An unanchored pseudo-narrator ('Odile'); an un-self-explained composer ('his'); musical motifs, music-making machines ('hidden melody', 'cogs', 'handle'); secrecy, hidden spaces, randomness ('key', 'a drawer', 'chance', 'mistaken'); disclosure, discovery, treasure ('unlock', 'unwrap', 'gift', 'oracles', 'homologies'); an omnivorous collector, especially of birds ('ghost of a bird', 'feathers', 'field notes'); despondency, despair, loss ('mourn', 'ashes', 'charred', 'ruined'). The crazy thing is that any of the words quoted in the parentheses might escape them or be exchanged with one or other of the preceding words and we'd be none the wiser. An *angel* recedes — into the book's future!

Interestingly, Glenny credits a threesome of non-poet, non-illustrator and non-publisher with putting together a pretty polished book of poetic non-poetry (it contains no verse).[15] This is key. Poetry shows that the things it is made of are floating points. Dis-locatings. The no-definite-thing-ness of things is what form ultimately defines.

Perhaps serendipity places Glenny's name at the head of this text? Displacement is its characteristic mode (there is no contents page). There are glossaries on obscure antiquarian themes ('the Nineteenth Century Novel: A Glossary of Terms', 'Footnotes to a History of

Birdsong'). Other sections are occupied mostly by empty space ('From Field Notes', 'Fragments and Notes'). More intriguingly, there are drifting footnotes to texts that are not included. Here's one:

> [5] Interiority was a spatial concept that relied on hidden rooms and cabinets. When she put her ear to the keyhole, the sound of ghostly minuets. (15)

And let me stop here, having sent *Bird Collector* into the ether (another rocket?) it already inhabits.[16] To say this book *wastes* time is to offer an idiomatic compliment. Aesthetics is a null set, vacuity's allure.

*

Postscript:

> What is the aesthetician
> But a mule hitched to the times?
> (Kenneth Koch, 'Aesthetics of the Aesthetician')

Subjectivity as the parent of orientation is under siege.

1   Cognitive psychologist Donald Hoffman cites Kurt Gödel's 'no theory of everything' and Georg Cantor's 'an infinity of infinities' in asserting that the world can never be adequately or finally described. He explains, 'Objects . . . have no definite values of physical properties, such as position or momentum when they are not observed', concluding: 'Our senses do not show us truths about objective reality'. Donald Hoffman, 'Fusions of Consciousness', *Entropy* 25, no. 1 (2023): 129, www.researchgate. net/publication/367000099_Fusions_of_Consciousness

2   A kinder explanation might be that representation, because it arbitrarily gives form, is misrepresentation.

3   Lawson argues that no objective world can be known because any attempt at objectivity is indexed to self-referentiality, especially in language, which is itself an artefact ('when you say something and it doesn't apply to itself'). He calls this 'the central flaw that undermines realism' . . . 'Products of a monist universe cannot be true or false, they merely exist'. Hilary Lawson, *Closure: A Story of Everything* (London: Routledge, 2001). See also 'Hilary Lawson on Closure', 7 June 2022, YouTube video, www.youtube.com/watch?v=Qh38Gaxg9tw

4   The ushering in of language poetry happened through John Cage and Jackson Mac Low — mesostics, aleatoric (chance) operations, the slicing and dicing of modernist as well as classical texts like *I Ching*. Theirs were among the first efforts to liberate the signifier and move literature away from external reference (Barthes' 'death of the author') towards autonomous relations within language.

5   Lauterbach explains: 'The world as such cannot be in the poems. Only language can be in the poems . . . [Poems] are about what might arise between the given and the chosen.' She approvingly cites Cage's 'turn art into life and life into art' and a reconfiguration of facts in an 'erosion of inwardness'. Ann Lauterbach, 'The Given and the Chosen — A Meditation', 11 February 2010, YouTube video, www.youtube.com/ watch?v=sZKPthDG7as

6   See note 1: David Hoffman in conversation with spiritualist Rupert Spira, 'The Convergence of Science and Spirituality (Part One)', 27 March 2023, YouTube video, www.youtube.com/watch?v=rafVevceWgs

7   Consider philosopher Martin Heidegger's idea of poem as 'dwelling', especially in the case of the poet Friedrich Hölderlin; or Ludwig Wittgenstein's point that language is incapable of describing what's outside itself; or Jacques Derrida's contention that meaningfulness ultimately implodes.

8   Of course, inception belongs to the narrative of *start–middle–end*. What we term the origin in Aotearoan poetry, generally attributed to the group of male writers who appear around 1930, is in fact a contrivance (see Roger Horrocks, 'The Invention of

New Zealand', *AND/1*, 1983), available at New Zealand Electronic Poetry Centre, www.nzepc.auckland.ac.nz/misc/horrocks.asp

9   Chris Tse and Emma Barnes, *Out Here: An Anthology of Takatāpui and LGBTQIA+ Writers from Aotearoa* (Auckland: Auckland University Press, 2021). Women have had it hard. For lack of them, Leigh Davis, co-editor of 1983's *AND/1*, adds an eponymous Anne Bland to the contributor list on the back cover. Five years later, in *Yellow Pencils: Contemporary Poetry by New Zealand Women* (Auckland: Oxford University Press, 1988), editor Lydia Wevers parades 28 real women poets to demonstrate what they are *actually* up to. Some 40 years on, Wevers' effrontery appears rather mild compared to the 200 women poets Paula Green features in *Wild Honey: Reading New Zealand Women's Poetry* (Auckland: Massey University Press, 2019).

10 From *Unpacking the Body* (1996), mixed media, in remembrance of Paul's daughter Imogen, who died in infancy.

11 There have been and are times when poetry approaches spiritual text. Cultures as diverse as Greek and Māori, in their founding narratives, commingle mundanity and the divine, another hybridisation.

12 Yuval Noah Harari, 'Yuval Noah Harari argues that AI has hacked the operating system of human civilisation', *The Economist*, 28 April 2023.

13 See my review 'Out Here', sidedoor, *remake8*, www.remakeight.wordpress.com

14 'The Propeller Club' seems pretty conventional when compared to her two published poetry texts.

15 Carrie Tiffany is the fabulous illustrator; Compound Press the outstanding publisher: https://soundcloud.com/paekakariki-fm/dinah-hawken-and-alison-glenny-poets-on-te-pae-24th-october-2021-192kbps. As an aside, I consider the deserved progenitor of open-textuality to be Anne Kennedy in *1000 Traditional Smiles* (Wellington: Victoria University Press, 1985), another work of woven time and floating protagonists (see John Geraets, 'Wholes in Part: Late Century Forays,' *Journal of New Zealand Literature* 34, no. 2 [2016]: 8–32).

16 Glenny's earlier collection *The Farewell Tourist* (Dunedin: Otago University Press, 2018) combines the same unfilled spaces and ellipses/strikethroughs, musical geological and naturalistic motifs, as well as cryptic sequences that contain proper names, listed footnotes to specified but unlocatable works, two appendices, etc. She comments: 'One of the things that appeals to me about the use of footnotes as primary text . . . is the invitation this seems to offer to readers to imagine their versions of what that missing primary text might be.' Alison Glenny, 'Poetry Shelf in conversation with Alison Glenny', NZ Poetry Shelf, 5 October 2018, https://nzpoetryshelf.com/2018/10/05/poetry-shelf-in-conversation-with-alison-glenny

Works Cited

Geraets, John. 'Out Here', sidedoor, *remake8*, www.remakeight.wordpress.com
'Wholes in Part: Late Century Forays'. *Journal of New Zealand Literature* 34, no. 2 (2016): 8–32.

Glenny, Alison. *The Farewell Tourist*. Dunedin: Otago University Press, 2018.
'Poetry Shelf in conversation with Alison Glenny', NZ Poetry Shelf, 5 October 2018, https://nzpoetryshelf.com/2018/10/05/poetry-shelf-in-conversation-with-alison-glenny
Bird Collector. Auckland: Compound Press, 2023.

Green, Paula, ed. *Wild Honey: Reading New Zealand Women's Poetry*. Auckland: Massey University Press, 2019.

Harari, Yuval Noah, 'Yuval Noah Harari argues that AI has hacked the operating system of human civilisation', *The Economist*, 28 April 2023.

Hoffman, Donald. 'Fusions of Consciousness'. *Entropy* 25, no. 1 (2023): 129. www.researchgate.net/publication/367000099_Fusions_of_Consciousness
in conversation with spiritualist Rupert Spira. 'The Convergence of Science and Spirituality (Part One)', 27 March 2023, YouTube video, www.youtube.com/watch?v=rafVevceWgs

Horrocks, Roger. 'The Invention of New Zealand'. *AND/1*, 1983.

Kennedy, Anne. *1000 Traditional Smiles*. Wellington: Victoria University Press, 1985.

Lauterbach, Ann. 'The Given and the Chosen — A Meditation', 11 February 2010, YouTube video, www.youtube.com/watch?v=sZKPthDG7as

Lawson, Hilary. *Closure: A Story of Everything*. London: Routledge, 2001.
'Hilary Lawson on Closure', 7 June 2022, YouTube video, www.youtube.com/watch?v=Qh38Gaxg9tw

Tse, Chris, and Emma Barnes, eds. *Out Here: An Anthology of Takatāpui and LGBTQIA+ Writers from Aotearoa*. Auckland: Auckland University Press, 2021.

Wevers, Lydia, ed. *Yellow Pencils: Contemporary Poetry by New Zealand Women*. Auckland: Oxford University Press, 1988.

Reviews

Claire Orchard

Claire Orchard
Liveability
Te Herenga Waka University Press, 2023
RRP $25, 80pp

Liveability is intoxicated with ordinary life — its overlooked joys, characters and paraphernalia. Right from the beginning, Claire Orchard sets out to make readers notice themselves and their strangeness. The first poem opens in a southern regional call centre. Outside, it starts to snow. The narrator pauses to watch the small flakes and begins to wonder:

> When exactly did we first notice water birds,
> so hearteningly unsinkable on lakes,
> first notice lakes?

A moment later they note:

> Half a gingernut drowned in my KeepCup makes no ripples
> only sinks without fuss and deep as joy sometimes does.
> ('Southern Regional Call Centre')

Slipped under the relaxed, conversational tone of these poems is Orchard's mastery of pace and movement. The poems have a hold-your-breath quality. The endings reveal themselves through sharp, poignant images or rounded revelations. Each one gives the sense that this author will explain the truth about life with care. She guides her readers through rough terrain with the gentlest of touches:

Be sure to hold hands at any crossroad, with the world
being in such a rush, and us being
unable to stop ourselves scratching.
('If you take one piece of advice this year let it be')

Orchard's exploration of the mundane comes across as survivalist — an
attempt to stay awake amid turmoil and drudgery. And things go wrong
in *Liveability*. A dog falls prey to a snake. A car crashes. There are small
frustrations and cavernous anxieties. Orchard examines them all with
a survivalist hope that never feels saccharine. On occasion, she comes
out with her pen swinging. 'All stations' critiques our pitiful efforts at a
climate crisis response:

We are putting the real work off in the boats
We are putting practical solutions off in small boats
. . .
This is *Titanic*
This is *Titanic*

It's a quiet condemnation. But things can't always be phrased with soft
edges. Sometimes she pulls the Band-Aid off fast and waits in the white
space for the fallout:

Just now I was driving with Geoff, he was
sitting right next to me in the passenger seat,
when a bullet pierced the windshield.
('The condition of knowing')

There is longing in all these poems. Often, a desire to find a balm for a
wound:

I've always hankered after
hydrangeas like my nana's, but they never grow well
for me, no matter what kind of shit I dig into the soil.
('Landscape')

Overall, the collection succeeds in finding readers a soft place to sit within the world. Without fanfare, Orchard proves the vital role of an artist. She cuts our dense world into manageable scenes, pries her readers' chests open just to dab something warm within the cavity. Her final piece begins:

> Breaking a soft, yellow heart
> with the edge of my fork, I recall
> the shallow earthenware bowl
> that always sat upon your windowsill.

And it ends, eyes still fixed on this simple beauty:

> still, serene, aglow with pale promise.
> ('Oh boy')

Hannah Mettner

Hannah Mettner
Saga
Te Herenga Waka University Press, 2023
RRP $25, 88pp

Dip your toes into *Saga* and the pages ripple blushes, crushes and scars. Hannah Mettner's newest collection is a flood of modern anxieties and experiences, explored through lush language and muscly images. It's easy to be swept up in the lines. 'If not nuclear' delves into its deep theme with a vivid first stanza:

> The old ladies of the supermarket
> rubbing my belly like a genie's lamp
> just to remember the lemon-barley
> edge of adulthood.

Mettner's poems are political, self-aware and unrelenting. There is something sensuous about them, too. Every line is one a reader can roll their whole tongue around. The phrasing is lyrically gluttonous — rich, sour and cutting on the swallow. Her language choices broil on the tongue. Words fizz:

> In this church the colours are fairy floss and hayfever and bubble-gum-
> flavoured milk but Byzantine.
> ('Birth Control')

Within scenes, Mettner does a masterful job of extending resonant images into webs of association. The perusal of church art turns to an examination of feminine experiences throughout history in 'Birth Control':

Seems like every initiation into womanhood is an initiation
into pain. Into seeing the other women
busying around us, bruising hips
on corners of tables, gasping
in the bathroom as their stitches tear —
trying to hold back the knowledge of it, doing their best
always, always rubbing honey into the wound, almond
butter into the cracks in their hands

And here appears the central tension of the book: Mettner feels that the
saga of life is one of pain. At the same time, it's rare and dazzling:

Stepping outside is like diving into
a chlorine-bright pool where everything
is hard and modern and floating.
('Anita')

Stripping away expected turns of phrase and representatives for real
emotion, she relies on stranger-than-fiction specificity to show life's
true nature. Details bristle from the pages: the 2000s' body chocolate
craze, Anne Carson books spotted in the wild, and second-hand
knowledge of Buffy the Vampire Slayer. This glut of knowledge presses
in on Mettner:

Nowadays, historians reckon van Gogh cut off his ear because he hoped
it might stop the roar of his tinnitus, not because he was mad.
('Guns, lots of guns')

Mettner also finds humour in her topics. This lifts the tone out of
morbid introspection. Titles like 'OMG, am I a hedonist?' or 'Love poem
with gratuitous sex' punctuate the collection. Moments of particular
tenderness and honesty are cut down to size:

All I want is another pair of earrings and
A deep emotional connection with someone
I enjoy fucking, is that too much to ask?
('OMG, am I a hedonist?')

Still, humour cannot hide the struggle of being a queer, creative woman
alive in our hustle-and-bustle world. The challenge to Mettner's artistry
appears again and again:

Art isn't work because it doesn't pay the rent. Sometimes I see all our
unmade things following us around like a haunted parade — van Gogh's
unsold sunflowers springing up around us.
('La bohème')

Despite all this, she finds herself back at work wading through the
questions that pester her. Can this be the substance of our lives? Can
our long sagas really only be complex middle chapters? The future
hesitates on the edge of the lines, unsure. The past lingers as scars in
bodies. Identity suffers the blows and transformations of time. Mettner
continues her poetic magic. She plunges her readers into singular,
touched moments where, as per the epigraph from 'Saga' by Mary
Ruefle, 'everything that ever happened to me is just hanging — crushed
and sparkling — in the air'.

Saga roars from the page. It's witchy and political. Hilarious. Heart-
wrenching. It made me want to gather up my skirts and pens and run.

Leah Dodd

Leah Dodd
Past Lives
Te Herenga Waka University Press, 2023
RRP $25, 94pp

I have been following Leah Dodd's work since I first
read 'hi-vis' in the third issue of *Starling*, in 2017, and so I was stoked
to see the announcement of this, her first full-length collection. *Past
Lives* glows with the warmth of the domestic, and an attention to
proximity. Poems pulse with the spaces between, between the sensory
details of the past, and the similes which in their playful originality
grapple with the now.

There are other spaces at work here, too: between pop-culture
references and the in-jokes of relationship, between memory and
imagination, between the leaves of 'cabbage trees [. . .] spiked with light'.
Dodd is in full command of her craft, and the formal shifts in the book
track feeling and hold voice. A sense of humour and play is at work,
and there is a strong sense that Dodd decides throughout the collection
exactly how close she wants the reader to be. The white spaces of
haunting in 'I am the ghost of the IKEA futon couch', the bustling
prose-poem closeness of the crowd in 'gig people', the 'waterfall' and
'slug trail' stream of imperative in 'how to astral project in a rental
bathroom' . . . the collection is one in motion, full of verb and verve,
exclamation and direct address. There is a sense of restlessness here,
too, of wanting, of prevailing movement. It's a collection interested in
change and transformation, of becoming 'a different animal altogether'.

The collection tracks the jewels and debris of girlhood, of found
family, of oven-burnt chicken nuggets, of climate change. Dodd carries
in her work a sense of the ironic and the discordant, the often-jarring
juxtapositions that characterise capitalism, and the way they live against

our skin. You will find Mozart and *Minecraft*, Keats and Club Penguin, Persephone and platform Pulps. Dodd writes with a keen eye for the hyperreal and the surreal, for the absurdity of our lives and times.

I finished *Past Lives* with a renewed apprehension of the thin lines between past lives and future ones, too, between life and decay and of beauty and loss pushed close. Poems like 'tether' and 'clucky' moved me with their simultaneous attention to tender firsts, and the sharp teeth that await them. Other poems, including 'Last Call Nigel' and 'walking to book club' stay with me for their sense of hushed awe.

Warm and striking, original and assured, *Past Lives* does not miss a beat.

Sarah Lawrence / harold coutts / Arielle Walker

Sarah Lawrence / harold coutts / Arielle Walker
AUP New Poets 9
Auckland University Press, 2023
RRP $29.99, 108pp

AUP New Poets is always a treat — each book containing three distinct chapbooks, connected by an erudite foreword by poet and scholar Anna Jackson. The *New Poets* collections are especially exciting, like finding the big prize on a scavenger hunt, after reading individual pieces often published in our essential literary journals, hearing work at bookshop readings, or at live and online festivals. I am glad of its continued return, and the role it plays in fostering emerging writers, offering us a heads-up about who to keep an eye or ear out for.

In *AUP New Poets 9*, which features the work of Sarah Lawrence, harold coutts and Arielle Walker, Jackson celebrates the distinct offerings of each selection while leaving the reader threads to follow through the book as a whole. She alerts us to key themes that include 'longing, fragility, romance and other tidal forces' and also highlights an attention to the past, as well as the 'dazzlingly contemporary present'. Indeed, alongside the contemporary and new I was delighted to notice references to the historic and mythic throughout these collections. These poems balance personal explorations of identity with wider explorations of this historical moment, of encounter and exchange, of embodiment and the forces that shape and challenge it.

Although perhaps relatively 'new', each of these poets writes assured, informed and formally accomplished work, and is at home in the spaces and ecosystems of Aotearoa, and indeed international, poetry. These are poets writing with an awareness of, and connection with, other writers:

essa may ranapiri, Airini Beautrais, John Milton. If someone wanted to know what is happening in Aotearoa poetry, this book is one of the first places I would point them.

We open with Sarah Lawrence's *Clockwatching,* a kaleidoscopic collection of poems which explore nostalgia and memory and contain a strong sense of searching. At times, these poems tumble forward over lines with a kind of breathless enjambment, evoking the sense of running, of unrestrained voice. And yet there is considerable craft in this selection, repetition serving to mark time passing, phrases echoing like memory. Jackson tips us off to intricate villanelle and slick sonnet work, and when I hit them, they were sure-footed, brilliantly executed — only deepening the feeling of the work.

Lawrence achieves a lot in these 21 poems, taking us through a lockdown, a train station, the Willis Street New World. Her settings are vividly rendered, shaped by love, confession and question, and the figures we meet in them are alive with desire, with disappointment, with confidence and vulnerability, with heat and risk. These are characters who live skin-to-skin, who carry humour into national emergency, who foster connection in the face of fragmentation and loss. Lawrence reminds us that there is music here, at the end of the world — Jack Johnson; Crosby, Stills, Nash & Young; Morrissey. *Clockwatching* is an accomplished, fully rounded and developed selection, and one of my very favourite reads of the year.

harold coutts's *longing* marks a distinct shift in the collection. Here the poet grapples with urgency and grit, taking on grand and timeless themes — god, flesh, death, grief — with a close eye on uneasy embodiment, bones and soil. Threat presses at the edge of many of the lines. These are poems with pulse, holding desire and lust, baptism and blade. coutts's voice is distinctive, tackling big themes using the lowercase form, their poems carrying an awareness of the ancient and the elemental into the contemporary.

In its attention to sound and form, its careful crafting and unflinching gaze, it reminds me of the powerful work of Liam Hinton, essa may ranapiri, Mark Prisco. I can see their work collected in a similar hardback treasure. coutts's work is entirely fresh, striking in its voice, frank in its stories. These are poems that tell it how it is, speaking right to the still-beating hearts of those of us who might recognise something of the dirt and haunted houses that lurk in poems like 'bad brain' and 'the limitations of my body are throttling me'.

coutts is a poet with a clear love for language, 'twixt and cutaneous, molten and crescendo, an awareness of where words can offer communion, and where they cannot reach. Yearning echoes here, and there are questions without final answers. Searching prevails, the speaker armed with candour and courage. This is a selection packed with startling and stunning lines, poetry at its sharpest and most essential, 'in blood crinkle communication'. I have my wallet ready to pre-order a full-length coutts.

Arielle Walker's *river poems* is lush and verdant, bringing affective attention to the lives that intersect in natural places. This is a fully-formed chapbook which holds together with care, tracing inheritances, imagining possible futures. Walker's poetry is rich in sound, and draws us close to an imperative voice that leads us with confidence through story, rivers, tikanga and dreams. Walker crafts satisfying connections throughout the selection, threading through recurring motifs, and using footnotes, titles and white space to add depth and poetic affect.

The poems negotiate contemporary challenges with an eye to the lessons of the past, and an awareness of issues of a much larger scale. The poem 'dream futures from a plant placed beneath your tongue' warns of the future we currently face, as well as one that is possible with a crucial and radical repositioning. A sense of liminality prevails, as with the children in the poem 'here are all the ways the story is the same', who are revealed in poetic footnotes to 'belong to both-worlds and neither-world / always caught inbetween'. Walker tracks nature and our role within it in a perpetual state of change and renewal, in flux, right on the cusp. 'In one future we remembered to look back, and to listen, / and things are good, and things are whole, and things are tika, / but that future flickers and is hard to see clearly through the / dreamhaze'.

I was deeply touched to read poems where Māori traditions met with Irish, and was held and taught by Walker's work as I researched words and ideas from my ancestors. This is poetry as balm, as whakapapa, as care. We find this emphasised in the central series at the core of the collection, 'rongoā', with its combination of cultures and places, languages and healing traditions. Ideas of collective care and interdependence ring through, as in another of my favourite poems, 'angiangi / feusag a' ghobhair', which opens with the line 'lichens are born from reciprocity'. This is a stunning selection that offers us hope in connection in the face of urgent need.

This latest in the *AUP New Poets* series has me seeking out the rest of the poets' work, eagerly awaiting their next offerings, and making space on my shelves for each of their full-length collections. Thank you, Sarah, harold, Arielle and Anna.

Alice Te Punga Somerville

Alice Te Punga Somerville
Always Italicise: How to write while colonised
Auckland University Press, 2022
RRP $24.99, 80pp

'I have been thinking about this advice.' This is the fifth line of the first poem, and it stayed with me until the last of the last: 'May I run out of ideas before I run out of time.'

Italicisation of foreign words has always seemed perfectly natural, and perhaps that's because I never thought to question the why of it. I was raised speaking English and only English; to italicise 'foreign' words was the principle dictated by the language I learned. The effectiveness of the inversion demonstrated by Alice Te Punga Somerville lies in its utter simplicity. English is the 'foreign' language here and it swallows the pages whole, resulting in any and all te reo *normalised as the standard, the default, and the to-be-expected.*

'Rākau' emerged early on as a favourite. There's an intimacy and flow of the language (ironically, in English) that pulled me in despite its short length. In fact, it's the brevity of the piece that makes it so impactful, lasting long after I had reached the end of the collection. And then to have it presented in te reo — *its intended tongue (even though I couldn't understand a lick of it) — drives this fundamental and complex duality home.*

'I have been thinking about this advice.'

This segues into 'red-carded', a sobering account of how even Māori *tend to differentiate between speakers and non-speakers. Between the biting and sombre lines, intertextuality is efficiently used to convey the humiliation of 'The Scarlet Letter' to that of an English-tongued* Māori *among a sea of their mother-tongued brethren.*

Honesty is expected in poetry, practically a given (this isn't a new-

found discovery), and to assume makes an ass out of u and me. Well, I must admit that I am an ass. When Alice taught me (yes, I was and still am her student), I was a little intimidated by her. And no, not because she's a wahine *(I grew up suffocated by loose-lipped, tongue-clipped aunties), but because I was intermingling with Indigenous studies when the only language I knew was imported.*

I was completely clueless that we were in the same boat (mainly because I rather expertly avoided the subject like it was a sinking ship), but now I know.

And now you know.

My bad.

Aroha mai.

'relative' is another poem that hit me hard; this time when I reached stanza three. It was the rapid-fire aggression and how that instantly ramped up after the previous stanza's repetition was broken down with each successive use of the line 'our poi make the sound of the horses which were met by children'. That sealed it for me.

This aggression struck a chord in me for its familiarity in hip-hop (with or without the hyphen) or 'rap', if you prefer. There's a certain phenomenon within the genre called the 'diss track', and much, if not all, of this collection has at least one foot rested on that curb. I'm not talking about the 'diss' in a pointed-attack kind of way, but in terms of energy (although some lines aren't afraid to get a little bloody).

Now, I'm not talking 'Biggie vs. Tupac' levels, where by the end both sides were dead on Channel One at 6 pm; think: '50 Cent vs. Ja Rule', a playful but devastating clowning rather than a series of drive-bys. Still, some of the lines do feel like an orchestrated hit — 'they're good people / i had a few of them work for me' or 'Do you talk to your landlord often?' It's the subtlety that has punch, and it's the subtlety that makes the doggish bites all the more satisfying to read.

Was this a long-winded way to mention rap beef in a poetry review?

Yes. Yes, it was.

Do you object?

Because if so . . .

Where do you think rap came from?

This is the epitome of aesthetics gelling with subject to create pieces that not only work and direct when recited, but work on the page itself as well. This collection is inherently working with a symbiotic relationship between theme and aesthetics-with-purpose because of the italicisation, and it serves as an effective throughline from the very first line to the last.

'I have been thinking about this advice.'

'Swipe left' puts the racy and touchy subjects within the self-evident confines of a dating app, which not only brings out a natural comedy in the piece, but, if there's a sure way to get kids (high-schoolers — you know, the future generation) into reading poetry, it's with this.

This point may be moot, because do kids even read poetry? I sure as hell didn't. In first-year undergrad I thought Dr. Seuss was a poet (and I still do, by the way).

In high school I would've used a choice string of adjectives to describe poetry that today would get me 'cancelled' (*note: consult 'urbandictionary.com').

And now I'm reviewing poetry.

A prime example of when ignorance is not bliss.

Funny that.

Either way, isn't that just like a Māori — using humour to mask vulnerability. Again, this ties back to that fundamental honesty we expect in poets and their work. But it also recalls a quality of storytelling common in Māori to add a little cheek in before the chin-check and you're left laid out on the front lawn.

Take 'mad ave', for example. We see high-schooler Alice wagging, the prick of a principal, and praying you don't encounter the neighbourhood menace (in this case, a dog) — experiences that everyone can relate to (the first one is applicable to me). And then comes the realisation that gentrification, by its very nature (as well-intended as it is), erases character from the neighbourhood in order to spruce up the joint and make it 'appealing'. It taps into the complexities of ownership, both in a literal sense and the more philosophical. I'll leave the final lines here (I assume you've read them):

i'm still not sure who has the right to mourn
who has the right to say
that their place was taken away.

There's that chin-check (consult UD).

I have been thinking about this advice
and I have decided to follow it.

Anthony Kohere

Jessica Hinerangi

Jessica Hinerangi
Āria
Auckland University Press, 2023
RRP $29.99, 76pp

There are no Māori mermaids
('Siren song')

Because something doesn't exist, does that mean a people, a culture, its lamp-bearers, should simply reject it? This idea of Māori mermaids (a fantastic mash-up, and Jessica's calling card) and its closest approximation, the marakihau, is prevalent throughout this collection. The idea of blending two distinct halves to form something culturally anachronistic (because of the endearing attitude of 'Why not?') may be blasphemous, and may bristle some britches with its apparent affront to, or lack of, tradition. But why not? Why should Māori shirk their interests in Pākehā things to stay 'pure'. Is there not a way to have both? Although the idea of seeing Barbie on a shelf in The Warehouse with a moko kauae makes me want to throw up, that's more of an issue about performativity. The idea that little Māori girls (and boys like my brother) playing with little brown Barbies in a piupiu seems a little . . . *queer* is because that's a targeted piece of plastic meant to capitalise off culture (and you thought I meant something else. Got ya). I suppose one must also pay to read these poems, but . . . money doesn't grow on the trees used to feed the printers. And I don't think artists actually like the 'starving artist' cliché. We like to eat. And eat *well*, I might add.
Anyway . . .
That's what I get from Jessica here. It's not about faceless marketing

teams analysing current trends of representation, it's about an individual's *self-expression*. And that's what poetry is about; I cannot think of a worse art form to be saddled with commercialisation (look at the state of cinema). Could you imagine manufactured poems? Template poems? AI poems? That might actually be worth a laugh around the wine-and-cheese table at slam night. I can see it now. The little beanies and beeswax beards. The black horn-rimmed glasses without a prescription. The freestyles that aren't freestyled because you're just throwing out random words. For example:

An	ee	thing
can	be	slam
man		if
you	say	it
like		this
(I	may	be
	ex	aj
je	rae	ting
	the	clee
shay.)		

Back to *Āria*.

I might have been remiss in my first reading of Jessica's work because I came away feeling a little disjointed. A little ambivalent. At times I felt I was peeking into someone's head a little too much. (God forbid poetry be personal.) There wasn't a single thing to grasp onto that I found familiar except the words on the page. The *language*. English (obviously) and te reo. Because I had read Alice Te Punga Somerville's *Always Italicise* beforehand, and because she puts forth such a compelling case as to why we (Māori) should treat all foreign languages as that, it made me read *Āria* a little side-eyed.

I found myself shaking my head and tsk tsk-ing all over *Āria* with disapproval. 'The two languages are blending together,' I said, '"and the mammy is almos—" Wait,' I paused, '"and the *mamae* is almost",'

I corrected. Yeah, it kinda ground my gears on the first read-through, having to stop and start, and decipher which words belonged to which language. But by the end, a baker's dozen (one-third) of the poems resonated with me. That's not indicative of the collection's quality as a whole — it's simply a result of the baggage I brought to the table. And that's what I got out of it. Not the whole pie, just one-third.

But that one-third . . .

One week went by and I hadn't written a single word in response. In comparison, Alice's review came together rather quickly in a day. By the second week, I sent that thing off to Tracey with an explanation for why I'd been dragging my feet with this. She replied in kind, but it was the prospect of having to return the review copy that kicked my arse into gear. Although not one word had been written, I'd found myself returning to *Āria* over the days and weeks since that first read-through. I'd crack it open to spy upon the blunt admissions and lines that wouldn't bugger off:

> I don't want to be moved around anymore
> I don't want to be touched by you.
> I want to
> touch myself.
> ('Barbie girl')

> I really needed to talk to you I thought it could just be us
> ('The Māori portraits')

> I saw my partner and his sister spit and I panicked
> and walked back to the car because auē, my mouth was dry still.
> ('Spitting on the statue of Captain Cook')

> there is no chance of sinking
> when their jaws snip gently at
> my nono.
> ('Eel dreams')

The earlier complaint I had about the blending of languages is moot. For this collection, for what it's expressing, it works to a T. This is what I've come away with from *Āria*: Why not form something from two distinct halves? Why not the fantastic mash-up? Why not have both?

I think it's kinda funny. Two or three weeks (who's counting?) I've sat on this collection not knowing if I'd even write a damn thing about it. Then, one email from Tracey expressing her understanding of my predicament (as well as, you know, sending the book back since I hadn't actually worked to keep it. I think I get to keep it now) and I've finished. I finished it in an hour or two (who's counting?). A simple, understandable action was the key to write this whole thing right now. And I'm glad I had nothing to say at first. I'm glad it took two or three weeks. Because some things need (or deserve) the time to gestate. To get good. No, I'm not referring to *this*. Quite the opposite.

I just didn't want to return the book.

Claudia Jardine

Claudia Jardine
Biter
Auckland University Press, 2023
RRP $24.99, 76pp

Biter is witty, effortlessly intelligent, and sexy — like the bisexual postgrad girl you meet at your first university party (but this simile could just be projection). There is extra joy in reading a collection when you know the poet is having fun. Jardine twines antiquity with modernity and goes where she likes, examining the silly, painful and significant moments which make up life — whatever century you are in.

As someone who loves classics but was never formally educated in them, beyond high school, it was a relief to discover there is no high-brow gatekeeping here. Jardine pulls the reader into worlds and stories she is clearly passionate about, and throws names to us until it feels as if we know them, too.

Throughout the collection, Jardine has included epigrams which she has translated from Greek, with some bonus creative licence. 'Irreverent' is one of those words Netflix likes to stick on anything vaguely quirky or interesting, but it definitely has a place describing the wonderful way Jardine treats these centuries-old works. Yet while we tend to imbue anything over a certain age with an ascending level of veneration, this often ignores the human universalities under which artistic work is created.

Art, particularly poetry, has long been an arena of play — for as many deaths of Dido, there is an Ovid wanting a threesome, or a Sappho imagining a good lay. I am unsure whether 'slap-assed' appears in the original Greek, but when Jardine uses it, in an epigram of the same name, there are definite twenty-first-century vibes. The poet is going back to the roots of these pieces, tugging on extant threads of sensuality which over time have been corroded by linguistic and cultural shifts. She engages in a sincere and spirited conversation with the original works, as opposed to imbuing them with a false sense of gravitas — which might take out all the fun.

'Field Notes on Elegy' is a gorgeous piece which shifts from karaoke to a jilted woman in a generic empire, then a melodramatic Roman, and settles on the Lady of Shalott. This again shows the evolution of playfulness in art, as Jardine flits through iconic literary eras, injecting humour as she goes:

> when we do meet
> I lose my mind for a minute
> briefly consider painting my name on a little boat
> and staging my own death
> float downriver just to hear you call me
> fair

I often feel we have left too much humour out of poetry. Jardine's collection is a reminder that we can be deep, while also having fun and talking humorously with our counterparts of yesteryear. Think the Sex Pistols doing a cover of 'My Heart Will Go On', or Britney Spears' musical rendition of *Beowulf*.

A poem which struck me with distinct tenderness was 'Thoughts Thought After Surveying the Contents of the Fridge', in which the narrator laments their father's inability to reseal a block of cheese. The piece is after Ogden Nash's 'Thoughts Thought After a Bridge Party', in which it is opined that women are unable to correctly open a package of cigarettes. Jardine's language is funny and sweet, with an underlying care:

> At home, only he can claim the title of Professor,
> but the way he opens a block of cheese
> is akin to unwrapping a bar of chocolate
> by putting it in the food processor

Other than striking a personal chord with me — my own father has woeful fridge etiquette — the piece shows Jardine's versatility. She is able to shift subject and tone without jarring the themes of the collection, she maintains an authentic voice, and she still manages to have fun.

This collection is a fabulous dare. It wants us to be passionate and cheeky, to follow our inner voice wherever it wants to explore, and to enjoy that process — and also to learn Greek and recline on a velvet chaise writing sexy poetry!

Sophia Wilson

Sophia Wilson
Sea Skins
ASM; Cerberus Press; Flying Island Books, 2023
RRP $10, 108pp

Sea Skins
Sophia Wilson

Sophia Wilson's first full-length collection brings together poems which sting, sit softly and run linguistic rings. *Sea Skins* is both clamorous and calm, embodying a land that will outlive us and will bear witness to the suffering of mass extinction. Human destruction resides within many pieces, sometimes as implicit threat, at other times as overt action — the mining corp moving in, or the mould in the room of a dying child.

You would be hard-pressed to find a recent poetry collection that does not touch upon climate change or the fears associated with it, but few do it with as much stark erudition. Too often we fail to do justice to the realities of climate disaster by not talking about it in terms of human intimacy. Too often we debate ozone in terms of percentages, or rising temperatures in decimal points, but do not actively explore these in humanistic terms. *Sea Skins* fills this void. A district has mountains made solely of 'small plastic labels' from rotting fruit ('The Evening Star'), and a narrator's children cry while handling 'small, charred animals' ('Unthinkable'). Chemicals leak through stanzas, killing bees and leaching into oceans where warm bodies still swim.

Wilson's collection is multi-faceted and luminous with the lives to which it speaks. It makes you look climate catastrophe in the eye, makes you inhale the ash and sulphur, while also handing you the hope and the potential inherent in human lives. The climate is felt through personal interactions and nostalgic wonderings, as a low hum or a deafening cry, an inseparable presence.

There is a supreme gentleness in Wilson's work that I adore. She can write white-hot rage and acerbic political commentary; however, there is never any doubt that she truly cares. At its heart, *Sea Skins* is made from a love for this world.

Belonging and not belonging, local or 'foreign' — these are counterpoints the poet looks at frequently, as the lines dance through countries, languages and time periods. When climate disaster comes to the fore, the question becomes larger. Is there anywhere we belong? Or are we succumbing to a slow, unerring erosion?

> the descendants are bagpipes, windpipes, piccolos
> altos, bull roarers, chimes, harps and river stones
>
> the descendants' vibrations are felt
> down railway tracks, on wire, in coal trucks . . .
> ('VI Robert Burns in stillness joins the movement')

Sea Skins has hope. With warm bodies made from the earth, we are inseparable from our planet.

David Simes

Jake Arthur

Jake Arthur
A Lack of Good Sons
Te Herenga Waka University Press, 2023
RRP $25, 72pp

I love old records because sometimes you can hear the needle scratching from the original recording. It happens a lot with jazz singles or recordings by blues artists thought to have been lost. The transfer process does what it can to remove the dust and debris stuck in the grooves. But for me, it's a way of capturing that raw feeling of a great piece of work, a sign that the songs surrounding the track, or its influences, are aching to be heard as well. Jake Arthur's poems are like this. Just off in the distance, you can hear the scratching of his influences, and the poems he's yet to write.

I'm quite jealous of Jake Arthur. Not just because he has a PhD from Oxford, or because, if his author photo is anything to go by, he owns exquisite jumpers, but also because his work flows so perfectly — all at once intelligent, humorous, revealing, confrontational and frankly delicious. As a reader of poetry, I am sometimes lost in the metaphors and similes jammed into stanzas, or when it seems that a thesaurus has been torn apart and pasted to the page.

The poems in *A Lack of Good Sons* remind me of the poems of Simon Armitage in a way: digestible, with every word choice evident. The textual references that Arthur uses come from every angle, from Renaissance ideas and *Teletubbies* to *Thunderbirds*. When describing the titular soft lips of the collection's thirteenth poem, a lesser poet wouldn't have described them as

Soft lips a pink overflow
in the Tubby Custard Machine.
('Soft Lips')

but it is exactly these references that play into the expanse to which Arthur is trying to respond. If it evokes the perfect image in the mind of the reader, then every reference is valid. He doesn't shy away from silliness, nor is he afraid to be political. He has poems about the derivation of 'grizzly' as an adjective for the bear, and one in which he thinks about a sasquatch on a dinner plate, while the poem 'Lads' delves into the privilege of masculinity, with its showmanship and 'boys will be boys' fantasy.

A Lack of Good Sons is a slim volume, but it evokes a sense of time that is worthy of a tome. Arthur slips between past and present; what would appear to be a mundane afternoon is juxtaposed with reworked legends. Perhaps the past and the present aren't so different after all? As Arthur writes:

> There is a sameness in everything.
> There is a terrible
> sameness to everything,
> is anyone else aware?
> ('1588')

Not everything is morose, though. The second poem in the collection, 'Hockey', shows the beauty and innocence of blossoming love. The protagonist attends a hockey game in which Rachel, a girl he admires, plays. The rhythm and onomatopoeia of Arthur's description of the game, matched with a brief embrace, is all about life's small victories, and how polarising these moments can be in our memories:

> I drive her home dazed
> by the yellow streetlights,
> her hand hot in my jean pocket.
> ('Hockey')

Or when Arthur's protagonist receives a love letter in 'Fleet', and:

So begins a sunshine interlude.
I am ringed with fronds
I am evolving vestigial organs:
webbed feet, a tail, a pouch
made only for dreaming.

These moments, which seem so absurd, are also striking, turning the unspeakable feelings of love into something tangible, ordained with the truest blessing of life. Reading 'Hockey' and 'Fleet', as well as other poems in this collection, you can't help but feel as if you're basking in the sun. You almost feel giddy with the thoughts of love, whether you've lost it or not. I read these two poems over and over. Short, simple and full of heart, they are the sort of poems you can dip into ad lib.

I've long had a fascination with swimming pools: the way the light reflects off the water, creating a sort of wet static; how you need to maintain it with filters or salt or a pool boy; and how rich men in films always die in them. So of course, I was instantly drawn to *A Lack of Good Sons*' cover, with its archival image of divers from the Hutt Valley Drainage Board at the bottom of the Naenae pool in Lower Hutt.

If I were to imagine Arthur's collection as a pool itself, I'd have no issues with jumping in headfirst, sinking to the bottom, and drinking in the water. Sure, it's full of chlorine, and perhaps the remnants of all the previous swimmers, but it's worth it. Arthur now ranks among the best poets for me. He has the voice of Armitage, the nuance and bite of Tim Key, the spit in the mouth of Freya Daly Sadgrove, and the slap and caress of Hera Lindsay Bird. Jake Arthur will prove to be an important poetic voice in Aotearoa, and I can't wait to see what he releases next. For now, I'll keep swimming in this pool, 'til the water's dried up and my fingers are pruned.

James Norcliffe / C. K. Stead / David Eggleton

James Norcliffe
Letter to 'Oumuamua
Otago University Press, 2023
RRP $25, 96pp

C. K. Stead
Say I Do This: Poems 2018–2022
Auckland University Press, 2023
RRP $35, 108pp

David Eggleton
Respirator: A Poet Laureate Collection 2019–2022
Otago University Press, 2023
RRP $35, 192pp

In the titular poem of James Norcliffe's new collection, the poet addresses 'Oumuamua — meaning 'scout' or 'messenger' in the Hawaiian language — believed to be the first known interstellar object to be detected in our solar system. First thought to be an asteroid, and later a comet, there was also speculation that perhaps 'Oumuamua was an alien technology powered by solar sails. Whatever it was, it did not linger, nor did it break the long galactic silence we have endured since we first looked up to the stars and began to wonder.

Letter to 'Oumuamua is rich in these silent visitations, these failures or refusals to communicate, to find one another in the darkness. 'The body in the bed' wonders at the weird interloper 'lying between us / or lying beside us, unmoving, peaceful', producing 'no anxiety, merely a mild curiosity'. In 'The search party', a narrator volunteers to join a search only to become enveloped in a fog which turns 'our torches against us' and disrupts the sonic pattern of their whistles to make direction elusive. The searchers have eyes and voices but still they cannot find each other, let alone the thing they are searching for. The poem ends with the narrator's disclosure that, 'beyond issuing our torches and whistles', the instigators of the search had never made clear what it was they were looking for. The poem is reminiscent of Kafka's short fiction: full of dark comedy, disorientation and missed connections.

Failing light, dusk, encroaching darkness — Norcliffe returns to these images again and again. The title of the poem 'Wolf light' refers to the hour as dusk turns to darkness, when a person might fail to see the difference between a dog and a wolf. In 'Knowing what we are':

It is dusk. Birds have gathered
on the shining mudflats.

Knowing what we are, they lift
into the air crying at our approach

The birds, like 'Oumuamua, like the poet, have a clearer sense of our nature than we do. In 'Kōtuku', the narrator imagines reproach in the look of two white herons standing in judgement of us for the warming earth, 'the relentless sun', 'the fires up north'. He is 'grateful to turn into the mist once / more, thick mist, swirling like guilt'.

Guilt and loss run through the book like a seam of coal. Norcliffe devotes an entire section, 'Really hot soup', to poems about climate change. People fail to appreciate the coming danger. They are in the soup, so they don't feel it getting hotter. They cannot see the tides rising as their hedges have grown too high ('Living in the entropics'), they are too busy worrying about the ethics of pet food to see 'that the sea is returning to the land / that the land is returning to the sea' ('Lambton Quay'). The sea also encroaches in 'The Granity Museum', set on the

West Coast of Norcliffe's youth, where the 'the surf roared / like a mill saw and cut / the coast away', and later swept the poet's childhood, preserved in a museum mason jar, away with it.

And then there is the poet's aunt in 'The coal range', her man long lost to the West Coast mines, as she 'places lumps / of coal on the kindling and sets the paper alight', obliviously playing her small part in the planet's heating, cooking her porridge on the range 'the Scottish way'. Perhaps 'Oumuamua would have some sympathy for her. A lonely widow now dead, along with her brothers, her village, and the coal which brought them all here. 'The coal range — long gone — sits / innocently, as a pan fries the last of the whitebait in fritters.'

C. K. Stead has been a prominent feature in the landscape of New Zealand letters since the 1950s. While studying for his Master of Arts at the University of Auckland, he and his late wife, Kay, lived in Takapuna and were regular visitors to the nearby home of Frank Sargeson; Janet Frame was then living in the hut at the end of Sargeson's garden. When the Steads later moved to Parnell, Allen Curnow lived across the road. Now in his nineties, Stead has outlived almost all of his contemporaries and many younger poets besides. It has been a long and fruitful writer's life, and these poems are filled with satisfaction in his craft, the whip of his words undiminished by age.

His new poetry collection *Say I Do This: Poems 2018–2022* finds him in an elegiac mood. Spurred on by a cardiologist's grim prognosis, he looks back on his life in Auckland, afloat on the dark water at Kohimarama beach at night. He remembers a chance encounter in Belsize Park in London, where he promises to say a stranger's name aloud in Paris the following day. In lockdown, he longs for the French Riviera.

The poems swarm with writers, their names dropping from his pen like autumnal feijoas: Hulme, Frame, Heaney, Adcock, Berryman, Murdoch, Murnane — all sweep across the stage of the poet's memory, receiving admiration, sorrow, aroha. There is, if you like that kind of thing, a vicarious thrill to be had in the intimacy of this 'brainy gossip' ('To be continued, perhaps'), as if we were permitted to eavesdrop for a moment on the conversations of these luminaries, both local and international.

Death is everywhere. In 'Mary', days after the funeral of the poem's subject, while 'swimming with my friend Geoff / at Kohi we met a whale at the yellow buoy'. The creature follows them, allows itself to be stroked. Stead sees it as 'Nature giving us a call / on the right side of silence'. Later, in 'A sonnet for Peter Wells', '3 orcas enter the harbour, a trinity, / a Sign perhaps, Peter, a fond farewell'. Here, as with Norcliffe's 'Oumuamua, the poet, in the absence of a god, calls on an intelligence other than our own to bear witness to the flickering of our existence.

As death nears, Stead is unsentimental and bullish in his atheism, even when these moments provide rare instances of a heavy hand among the deft intimacies of his more personal poems. 'The Challenge' reflects on the burning of Notre Dame in Paris in 2019:

> . . . science gets it right.
> Prayers go unanswered and a Christian learns
> His God is silent while Our Lady burns

Perhaps Stead has earned the right to be a touch clunky when his dander is up, and the world's stubborn refusal to part with its religiosity seems to irk him right up until the end.

As he puts it pithily at the beginning of 'Psalm of Judas, 4': 'He was not my shepherd / nor did I want one.' We can hear the psalms drifting behind the lines as we often hear snippets of other verses just beneath the surface of Stead's poems. Just as with the parade of writers that appears in this collection, here, too, is evidence of a writer's life well lived.

Stead is a former poet laureate and David Eggleton is another, and in his new volume *Respirator: A Poet Laureate Collection 2019–2022* we can see some of the faultlines that have opened up in New Zealand poetry (and in New Zealand society) over the past few decades. The very fact of Eggleton's laureateship shows how far New Zealand poetry has come since the old boys' club of the 1950s and 1960s. A performance poet of mixed European, Tongan and Rotuman descent, without so much as a university degree, Eggleton could hardly be more different to Stead, the grammar-school educated academic.

Eggleton has little in the way of filial reverence for his predecessor. In 'Dear Reader (Thoughts after reading CK Stead's poem "That Derrida who I derided died")' he sets about dragging the old poet from his chariot:

> wants his poems to shine out like good deeds,
> plain as common sense in a naughty world.
> CK Stead, CK Stead, was it something I said?
> Are you vexed I said you must deconstruct the text?

Now, if you're a fan of a bit of old-fashioned handbags-at-dawn-poetic-brouhaha, then this sort of thing is gold dust. But beyond the fun of the heaved hatchet there are real themes at work here.

Stead is a good faithful modernist in the English/Anglo-Irish/Anglo-American tradition. Like many of his contemporaries, here and elsewhere in the anglosphere, he has little time for critical theory of the dangerously French variety as embodied by the likes of Derrida. Stead wants a spade to be a spade, a poem to be a poem, a blackbird to be a blackbird; 'Not for Stead the paralysis of analysis, / he gets out and does, he socks it to the man.'

Eggleton is a very different proposition. Not for him the stark simplicities of the mid-twentieth-century New Zealand canon. Eggleton's poems are dense, polyrhythmic, eclectic things. They surprise and baffle. Reading 'Hone', I'm reminded of the sensation of running down a steep and uneven slope, the feeling of being propelled forward by gravity's own agenda. The words and lines clatter together, pulling you down the page. Rhymes are thrown into your path like potholes, pulling you up short or stretching out your hamstrings to their elastic limits.

> Poet of the rhododendron rodomontade; poet of AA.
> Poet blundering like a fat moth into the sunshine.

> Poet with a voice growly as a possum, chewing through
> Orsman's *Dictionary.*

It's dangerous, it's difficult, it's fun. What does 'rodomontade' mean?
I don't know, and I don't have time to look it up because the poem is
pushing me onwards.

While Stead is still tapping his foot to the steady rhythms of Yeats
and the intricate pizzicato of Wallace Stevens, Eggleton's ears are tuned
to a broader frequency. Here and there you can detect the proto-hip-
hop of Gil Scott-Heron, the snarl of John Cooper Clarke, the dub poetry
of Linton Kwesi Johnson. Perhaps beneath all that you can just hear
the drums of the Fijian islands where Eggleton's mother was born and
where the poet spent part of his childhood.

Even though he can quote the Euro-Western canon with the best of
them, Eggleton's poems are filled with allusion to popular culture, to
pop songs and punks, and to the myths, poetry and waiata of the Pacific.
His poems are often spells and incantations, demanding to leave the
page, to be rolled around in the mouth and spoken.

> Inside whale bone, shark tooth,
> inside shark tooth, dog fur,
> inside dog fur, albatross wing,
> inside albatross wing, kiwi feather,
> inside kiwi feather, kākā claw,
> inside kākā claw, whale bone.
> ('Circle')

Eggleton is no son of Sarge 'tapping typewriter keys, / ivory towers
making hay bales into learned academese' ('Sargeson Towers'). Rather,
he is the roguish uncle to a more diverse, less white poetry landscape,
a landscape that is home to the likes of essa may ranapiri, Hinemoana
Baker, Ruby Solly and Tayi Tibble. Eggleton's is a poetry of protest, of
pomposity-pricking, of the Pacific. A poetry that is a threat rather than a
comfort to the status quo.

Hazel Smith

Hazel Smith
ecliptical
Spineless Wonders, 2022
RRP $29.99, 138pp

ecliptical is several books in one in which
interdisciplinary creative practice researcher, educator and new media
artist Hazel Smith brings together a sprawling, densely rich collection
of works. Ranging between varied styles, voicings, tones and formal
justifications, and alternating between portrait/landscape formats,
Smith presses persistently and playfully at the possibilities of what
poetry on (and off) the page can be.

A musician, artist and academic, Smith writes with more than words,
and is attuned to and interested in noise. Appropriately, the collection
generates a sonic ambience of its own, while maintaining a precise
linguistic specificity within each poem. Clocking in at over 130 pages,
ecliptical is deftly ordered into six sections; each loosely themed,
enabling a gentle structure to what could otherwise be an intimidating
read. 'Bigfoot', in the penultimate section, states what could be
considered Smith's intention: 'joints are the points of articulation
needed / to advance the looser argument / otherwise thinking would
only be a mess of limbs'.

Smith's interdisciplinary practice means that countless poems are
written in reference to other works, and some were composed as part
of new media artworks accessible online or in film projects. As such,
there is a world beyond the book, and almost all of the pieces are
intertextual, allusive or hyperobjects, textual matter that is mattering
both simultaneously about and of media, as they say, *in media res* — in
the midst of things.

Part of me wishes to resist calling Smith's works 'poems' — in their allusive, intertextual reachings they seem to be confounding that definition; they live beyond the page. However, this would reinforce a conventional definition of what a poem might be, which is what Smith hopes to unpack and subvert. In 'Fractals': 'she began the poem again and again / in the hope of redesigning its symptoms'.

The book's literal sprawl is more than just stylistic — it ranges through complex issues of contemporary life as weighty as migration, displacement and systemic brutality (as in the section titled 'not for the delicate') with sensitivity, alongside intimate lyric sections and often comical musings on creative process. While moving with ease from expansive prose poetry to densely compressed clutches of words that play sonically with powerful caesura and ellipses — the absences and fragments alluded to in the book's title — Smith honours their commitment to 'embrace amputations / rather than the whole body'. Indeed the book's opening piece, 'The Collection', introduces the text-as-body image which hangs the book's bones together. The guidance provided by this piece is crucial for the reading of *ecliptical* as a whole: 'she wondered if the poems / needed to add up [. . .] / pondered whether it mattered / what positions they took / at the volume's table'.

This image of the 'table' raises the notion of decentralising power that is key to the themes and formal functioning of the book: what stories, whose stories, and how are they told? Smith is all too aware of the infinite possibilities hanging from the conventional understandings of both 'book' and 'writer', and is sensible to outline and frame her intentions, expectations and how they might be met or subverted throughout the process of reading.

The political imperatives of *ecliptical* are ambitious and bold; Smith approaches, with an unblinking gaze, complex global warfare and violent displacements and brutalities (both contemporary and historic) committed against a number of minority communities and individuals. Her sensitive, rigorous exploration of such should be applauded. However, with the density of the collection and the world's plethora of griefs and injustices (as explored in the sections 'not for the delicate' and 'passport without destiny'), I do find that the sheer number of works (nearing on 60), and particularly the heavy subject material, leave me longing for — to put it simply — fewer words.

With its multi-pronged methods, wide-reaching subject matter and playfulness of form, is it possible that this book is doing too much? It is a remarkable feat, which I fear runs the risk of losing itself (or I, myself?) in its multiple threads — and yet this keeling over, this maximalism, this embracing of amputations at the expense of the singular body, might just be the point.

ecliptical vibrates with an invigorating ambience of multiplicities, a wide-reaching network of information that hums in and of our contemporary worldings. In this sense, one can dip in and out via various points of access, its detailed notes section also replete with hyperlinks to tantalise the reader who can't resist a rhizome.

And so, the collection does exactly what it sets out to — it jolts, hums, shouts and whispers, resists linear (and page-bound) reading, and, as such, reflects Smith's acclaim as an artist and thinker in sonic and musical terms and temporalities. Impressive in its vastness and stylistic range, it is evidence of Smith's advocacy for writing as experiment, as play, as process, as well as a site for/of worldmaking and sociopolitical inquiry.

Ila Selwyn

Ila Selwyn
slipping between
Masque Media, 2022
RRP $20, 90pp

The essence of *slipping between*, a poetry collection by Ila Selwyn, is captured in a stanza from 'the great leveller':

> i grab time by the balls
> try to make it dance
> before my time runs out

I read this collection as a dance, choreographed scenes of a rich life. Birds and butterflies, flight and dancing suggest an energetic free spirit and a desire to be physically unrestricted and uninhibited.

Selwyn's first poem, 'trapped', perhaps reflects her own feeling of being 'pinned to the page'. And there is a sense of doom and desperation in the lines:

> as soon as we leave the womb
> we're destined for disaster
> ('slicing the lines')

She does not shy away from heartache and betrayal in 'hand-me-down women', 'private sorrows' and 'notes rising from a bamboo flute' for example, but nor does she focus on negativity. She writes:

> peel back the anger
> fill with flowers
> ('notes rising from a bamboo flute')

Overwhelmingly, there is a sense that the poet wants to snatch each moment and make the most of it, to pack as much into her full life as she can before 'disaster' strikes.

I won't contemplate the meaning of the final poem 'eroticism in a first time fired gas kiln' which is part music, part furnace.

Selwyn is not afraid to call on the poetic devices of our ancestors—the imagery, alliteration, assonance and rhyme which make her poems accessible, musical, memorable. For example,

> cloud faces morph in moments
> leap over a train to town
> track a man in a black fedora
> smoking a cigarette
> red reflecting off
> a wet window of words
> ('a cold cryptic night')

and,

> high heels on the concrete
> staccato to his heavy beat
> ('entangled in his breath')

The cover illustrations of svelte nymphs and the pencil drawings which accompany the poems, also the work of the author, help tell this story. The marks in her quirky drawings have a sensitivity and gentleness about them and her subjects have the grace and energy of a dancer.

Jan FitzGerald

Jan FitzGerald
A question bigger than a hawk
The Cuba Press, 2022
RRP $25, 72pp

The cover image of *A question bigger than a hawk*,
a hand-printed linocut by the collection's author, is of a person
simultaneously being dropped and rescued, falling and being saved —
or flying like a bird. Apt, given that the anthology's title is taken from a
poem in which FitzGerald realises 'I've been living with strangers!':

> Chased by a question
> bigger than a hawk
>
> ......
>
> 'Am I adopted, too?'
> ('A question bigger than a hawk')

The theme of adoption, and the struggle to come to terms with all it
entails, runs through the collection. But from the outset, the poet recalls
the shared intimacies of a close adoptive mother–daughter relationship.

They spend a penny in a 'Ladies restroom, 1950s', where 'women
dab nail polish / on laddered stockings' and '*mmmmmm*' their cupid's
bow lips together. The hats, the heels, the perfume sprayed on the back
of the hand and 'the dead fox slung around her neck' are as vivid as
yesterday. FitzGerald ends the poem:

> And we walked down the street laughing,
> two women, hand in hand.

We learn of the poet's deep connection with the natural world in her 'tom-boy hideaway' catching birds for company in a strawberry frame with

> beards of lichen tufting
> from silvered wood.
> ('Bird catcher')

In poems as vivid as a box of home movies found in the attic, FitzGerald introduces us to the colourful characters she's met across her lifetime, like the town-renowned artist Reverend Sanders who was caught creating 'His own version of paint by numbers' with the Sunday school slide projector,

> or old man Dalton, church elder and recovered alcoholic,
> telling the new communion boy
> there were sixty pours to a bottle,
> and when he died, the boy poured seventy-five, straight.
> ('Reverend Sanders')

We meet Mr De Rossi the window washer, who has 'glasses thick as encyclopaedias' . . . 'pressed against a window like a gecko'; the unnamed man who brought her the 'perfect balance between submission and desire'; people with umbrellas walking heads down 'like dogs at their dinner plates'; and the kuia who 'shoot puffs of smoke / out the side of their lips', 'knock their pipes / on the bottoms of their shoes', and give her money for ice cream. FitzGerald has a painterly gaze:

> Light has wandered through
> with a Van Gogh paintbrush,
> beach chair and easel under arm,
> stroking the gazanias.
> ('Empty section')

She asks:

> Could anything be colder
> than a lube bay on a frosty morning?
> ('Mechanic')

Perhaps the answer is in a cut pumpkin:

> I have slit your skin,
> severed your stalk,
> scooped out your slippery seed.
> ('Pumpkin slicing with Sylvia Plath')

We read of enduring love and the struggle for sobriety, the power of mother nature and man's destruction of it.

In the final poems of this perhaps cathartic collection, we hear the crickets and uncertainty of Covid-19 lockdowns, but FitzGerald claims for herself:

> The night, a book,
> and the slow pleasures of age.
> ('Winter nocturne')

FitzGerald has deservedly been twice shortlisted in the Bridport Prize, and this fourth collection shows she still has much to share.

Vivienne Ullrich

 Vivienne Ullrich
We came from Hamburg
The Cuba Press, 2022
RRP $25, 80pp

Retired Family Court judge Vivienne Ullrich KC chronicles her husband Phillip's family history from 1920 Hamburg to 2004 New York in this her first published collection of poems.

Phillip's Jewish grandparents lived in Hamburg in the 1930s, when the German Reichstag was controlled by the Nazi Party. In 1938, as war appeared imminent, his grandmother, Wally Simon, put her 13-year-old daughter, Liesl, on a Kindertransport to England to escape threat and persecution. Later, both Wally and her son, Eric, managed to escape to England too. Not all of the extended family were so lucky.

Ullrich's poems, built on extensive research and imaginings, explore the theme of exile — from family, community and country. The first of the 36 poems introduce Phillip's great-aunt Erna, who abandoned her husband and three daughters and was never again spoken about. Ullrich approaches the poems from the sympathetic view of a Family Court judge who has heard many reasons for women's seemingly inexplicable actions. In 'Erna', Ullrich speculates about Erna's life, and then about what might have caused her behaviour in 'Anyone who knew'. She tells us the 'daughter above rubies' dies 'alone, nursed by nuns'.

The second section, 'Hamburg 1936–1943', imagines Wally confronting the 'vast desert' of widowhood. Ullrich shows tension escalating both within and outside the family. In 'After Kristallnacht', she walks us, 'glass shards kibbling under her soles', to the station, where she leaves Liesl with other children in 'Kindertransport'. Ullrich uses details like 'Two toddlers [who] have their potties tied with string' waiting alone at the station to represent the horror of separation for both the children and their parents.

Ullrich imagines how each of Liesl's omas (grandmothers) contemplated suicide. 'Oma [Alice Rosenbaum] had neatly cross-stitched cyanide / into the hems of her dresses . . .' Her paternal oma lies down

in a comfortable bed in my own house
under the quilt Zelda sewed for me
within hearing of my little carriage clock.
('Oma Nathalie Simon')

Defiant, Wally manages to ship her possessions out of Germany, but they are lost when the ship sinks.

In the section 'England 1938–1942', a penniless Wally escapes to Britain, where she is reduced to becoming a lady's companion who 'pours tea at three' and labours to 'deadhead herbaceous borders', but she is reunited with her children. 'Carapace' describes Wally 'trafficking her widowhood for / refuge in New Zealand'. When she leaves Liesl in England and takes Eric to New Zealand, she gives Liesl a prayer book 'To keep her safe and grant her peace', until she, too, sails to New Zealand.

The fourth section, 'New Zealand 1943–1955', tells of the family's struggle to integrate in a foreign land. Finally, in 'Wellington to New York 2003–2004', Phillip reunites with his extended family.

They had not been murdered.
They did not bear a tattooed number.
But they carried the debt of survival.
('Diaspora')

The poems are a family gift, generously shared — including photographs, a family tree and contextual afterword — which can be appreciated by all as a reminder of the Holocaust. Through Ullrich, we feel the plush of a Persian carpet under our feet, the sting of a slap, the rip of separation and exile. She takes us there.

Louise Wallace

Louise Wallace
This is a story about your mother
Te Herenga Waka University Press, 2023
RRP $25, 88pp

From the get-go this collection exploring pregnancy
and new motherhood disrupts the idea of the maternal, the domestic
as uninteresting, straightforward, underserving of creative space or
existential inquiry. After all,

> This is a story about your mother.
> Just like every other story.
> ('Vessel')

I am obsessed with the book's cover image and how it speaks to what
the poetry is doing. Like two friends talking. An oh-so-familiar scene —
a bathroom awash with objects that have clashed with life, skin, a child,
a naked mother. Domestic debris that holds and is held. Like Wallace's
poetry it is at once awry, real, sublime. I find myself coming back to rest
and wrestle in the image, seeing, thinking, feeling different things with
undulating perspective because of where the poems take me, places
where an unborn baby is

> a blueberry the size of disbelief
> ('Congratulations')

> and where
> it knows   everything it knows centuries   beyond you
> ('Have confidence in fibre')

The second of two opening poems, 'Yesterday' (after the Beatles song) contains the anger and ache of a mother-to-be in the process of losing a father in mental decline.

> my father my child the gentle person   we knew
> ///
> photos on the mantel   dad young sharp   and vibrant I used to love
> finding cicada shells their thick   skins the best ones I'd keep   in old
> matchboxes treasures   artefacts   but I don't *want*   an artefact
> sometimes   life *is* terrible sometimes

'Yesterday' is devastating and affirming, a reminder that we are born and we die in shifting, messy relational bonds of need and care — concentric stories that overlap, separate, contain and 'tell' each other. As I move through the book I take this poem with me, those three tender slashes / / / — the father turned child, the daughter turned mother, the unborn child and grandchild. As a reader I've been made a vessel among vessels. I must carry the three of them with me.

The second sequence, 'Like a Heart', made up of 40 poems — one for each week of pregnancy — is the breathless, thrilling, funny, uncanny body of this collection. As a mother myself, I immediately feel both unmoored and woven in. Questions percolate. How to be a mother, partner, lover, daughter, writer? The familiar doubt, fatigue, the anticipation and the strange actuality of becoming and being a mother — at the mercy of a host body where

> reason is now held in your nipples and inaccessible
> ('Pep talk for a sap')

I love how this sequence speaks embodied truth to what it is to be a mother now, in a world where parenting advice isn't just dispatched by well-meaning relatives but at scale via the market, corporate brands, the internet. I revelled in learning that these poems were created with lifted text from the Huggies week-by-week pregnancy guide — marketing

content for consumer mothers — filtered, manipulated, edited through
the human mother, through the rogue body, through a subconscious
that is

        a deformed mother

    a creep with strange hair
        flooding

        your mind
          pruning off

    common sense
    ('Your subconscious is')

to give us something altogether more real, reassuring, valuable —
poetry that pulsates *like a heart.*

And indeed, this is poetry beholden only to its own form, in which
the shape, the rhythm of each poem on the page makes emotional
weather, marks emotional terrain. The pause, the gap, the connection.
Poems that chafe, ruminate, fragment. A poem might be both fractured
and contrarily connected by an x, a blank space, a comma, a slash or a
full stop.

Somewhat baby-brained, I reach the final slender section of the book
— a single poem, 'Vessel'. A letter, a gift, a story from mother to son.
Something has shifted here. The mother is now an 'I' speaking to her
child as 'you'. Separate and connected. This is a voice moving towards
and speaking from inside the bond.

We knew who you were as soon as we saw you
The second they pulled you from my body
The name means firm or strong, and you are beautiful.

There are things here that are known to the mother now — the pain of childbirth, a name becomes a person — and there is a kind of raw, eudaemonic clarity, a stillness in the eye of the storm. I feel it in the form of the poem which oscillates between short, plain-speaking prose stories and open, gently suspended words and lines in white space.

> There are many different scales of pain
> Some are songs
> > Some linen
>
> > with white lace trim.
>
> ('Vessel')

In the end, I am not sure for whom I am weeping — this mother, all mothers, myself — but I am weeping. And I will be giving copies of this sublime, beautiful book (and perhaps a box of Huggies) to all the new and not-so-new mothers I know, with a card that says

> keep congratulating yourself honey you're doing a great job
> ('Small and reassuring interactions with your mother')

Michele Leggott

Michele Leggott
Face to the Sky
Auckland University Press, 2023
RRP $35, 92pp

and so the daughter library
remakes itself and is not lost
though great libraries burn and cities fall
always there is someone
making copies or packing boxes
writing on the back of a painting or a photo
always there is someone
awake in the frosty dark
hearing the trains roll through and imagining
lying under the stars at Whakaahurangi
face to the sky on the shoulder of the mountain
between worlds and mirror light
('Very fine lace knitting')

This extract, taken from 'Very fine lace knitting', captures the senses of
loss and salvaging, of hope in isolation, and of observation, distanced
yet skin-close, that are at the centre of *Face to the Sky*, Michele Leggott's
eleventh poetry collection. Grounded in the experiences of two women,
separated by history yet bound by place, this collection traces key
moments in their lives, delicately weaving along with their words the
gaps, gentle and violent, that frequent our stories.

Comprised of six sections containing three pieces each, despite
being firmly tied to place, this collection thrives in movement. From the

opening section of 'early morning cloud', the emotional stakes continue to build along with changes in weather — from the gentle grief of 'light winds at first', Leggott moves us from the mourning of distanced family in 'scattered showers' to the medical fears of 'gales in exposed places' and the sad forward motion of acceptance in 'isolated heavy falls'. To close, in 'changes across the region', Leggott creates a careful portrait of self across time in 'The workbook', a fresh harmony of voices in 'Iridescence' and, finally, the settling of hope beneath the watchful slopes in 'Whakaahurangi'.

The more I return to the layered intricacy of *Face to the Sky*, the more I notice what I have missed — it continues to give more with each reading. This is fitting for a collection invested in a calculated shaping and reshaping of story and semantics, words freshly fizzing even — perhaps especially — in repetition. Each piece dips between voices, as words from a century past are rubbed out and smudged back into new forms with new, unexpected resonances, at times comforting, at others unsettling and discordant. This is the art of mesmerising words from the air, flickered and morphing, frozen for a moment then changed/ gone/rewritten, as is clear from the first piece of the collection, 'Konene | Wayfarers', which welcomes the collection in beneath the watchful observation of the Peter Buck memorial, where there is:

a shutter clicking open
a shutter clicking closed
close enough to touch
blue and black and iridescent
a word the five year old will meet in time   wingbeat | featherfall
and pull towards the moment   wingbeat | featherfall
a long time ago

This close observation, the photographic click of the shutter, is present throughout, as is Leggott's returning investment in the iridescent, in the capturing of new perspective, moments caught in constant 'retrograde motion', in 'collapsing memory', in 'the copy of a copy'

('Dark Emily'). Stories arise from the land and sea, overlapping and polyvocal, Somerset collapsing into Huatoki, the rolling ship, the rolling black sands, the rolling rhythm, the violent underlying thrum of colonial intrusion beneath the domestic. Yet, even where pieces reach across borders of time and continents, into 'nightingale infinity / sour cherry momentum' ('A Vida Portuguesa'), they remain held in steady observation, grounded in the strangeness of the present.

In 'A Vida Portuguesa', we witness the gentle tragedy of families spread distant, 'a door that opens / a door that closes / a door a door and a door'. Saramago pivots to Lady Gaga as 'the party in the street echoes between stone walls', in the space of reconnection and partings, where we become doubled, both 'that lucky confluence of travellers in the corner of a crowded room / hoisting a glass to the future', and simultaneously haunted by the retrospective knowledge of encroaching 'pandemic darkness'.

Increasingly, we find intersections of the micro and macro, the personal and the global. This is perhaps most evident in 'Walks and days', where we see the collision of 'lines of traffic' that 'snake around testing stations' with 'the good and faithful dog curled on her bed / paw the same familiar shape but the paws are cold'; where the image of 'Taliban fighters' who 'sit in the Presidential Palace / in Kabul this morning' becomes intertwined with 'a 3–4 mm growth enough of a worry to fast-track admission'. Following this, in the blood poetry of 'Haemopoiesis', the 'ghosts of the house' share space in 'a new body / a soul the shape of an oar', caught in the violent dance of waiting, the blending of art and medical in the patient's navigation of diagnosis.

Yet even in the loneliness of treatment, the present is never entirely disconnected from the past, instead coming into 'contre-jour' focus, solidified in shadow against the brightness of an ever-watchful past, stepping 'those gaps between worlds' ('White-flowering mānuka and pōhutukawa'). Throughout *Face to the Sky*, Leggott explores the bittersweet nostalgia of lives that are, were, were never, and could have been. This is a work of grief and fear, but, above all, of profound hope: in essence, one which is ultimately and profoundly human.

Koenraad Kuiper

Koenraad Kuiper
Garments of the Dead
Quentin Wilson Publishing, 2023
RRP $37.50, 208pp

Koenraad Kuiper emigrated to New Zealand from the
Netherlands in 1951, and has published four previous collections of
poetry. *Garments of the Dead* is arranged in 15 sections, each running
as short sequences on the same theme — 'Pictures', 'Tales', 'Addresses',
'Epigrams' and 'Elegies', to name but a few.

The book is prefaced with a page that Kuiper has called 'Credo'. It is
worth quoting a few lines here, as they reveal both the technique and
the thinking behind the collection:

> Words have rhythms and sound patterns. Poems are inter-penetrations
> of rhythm, sound and images, as Paul Hoffman used to say. My poems
> must have sound patterns that are right for the imagery. The rhythms
> must be taut. The tension of the lines must not become the lesser
> tension of prose. If words are to count, then you have to watch for
> clichés. They make poems easy to read but it is not the task of the poet
> to make reading a poem easy.

After the 'Credo' comes a section which Kuiper addresses to his own
poems, beginning 'My poems regularly wake at sun up. / They are
fastidious dressers. He imagines six of his poems travelling on the
shinkansen, the Japanese bullet train, silently facing one another across
the compartment.

> The early morning suits them.
> They are waiting for the clear autumn light after the

dawn
which is always changing
and for which you must rise early.

They were once good church people.
They knew their creed, said grace
and discussed sermons

but now they are no longer in search of an author.
They sit in lotus position on the long seats
that you can reverse when the train reverses.
('My poems', 'ii')

The second section is called 'Home', and includes three poems recalling
the stark lives of Dutch grandparents. Each of these three is followed
by a version in Dutch, a pattern which repeats occasionally throughout
the whole collection. Sometimes there is a page in Dutch, once or twice
in German. The poems were written in a variety of languages and then
translated back and forth — English to Dutch or Dutch to English.
At first, I tried to read the Dutch versions, to listen for their sound
patterns, but my ignorance of aspects of the pronunciation hindered my
enjoyment. What to do with so many 'j's, 'z's and double 'o's?

Only one of the chapters has a non-English title — '**erfdeel** (*delen*) o
portion, heritage; *vaderlijk* ~ patrimony' — and it is perhaps one of the
most curious. It begins with:

Sometimes, post-war, I lie
at night sweating and hear
in the distance the sirens
and the drone of heavy bombers
and wake devastated.
('i')

The second poem begins with the line 'Hitler and I go back a long way.' We consider the evolution of his moustache from a wax-pointed twiddling monster to the one that everyone recognises, as the razor moved ever inwards. We consider the relationship between Adolf and Eva, and see their final days in the bunker. It is an odd memorial of unsettling and uncomfortable images.

Kuiper's collection is constantly full of changing images. So often they are drawn achingly well. In the section called 'Benedictine sonnets', one of my favourite poems, 'ii', contains this wonderful evocation of a watchmaker:

The watchmaker at 287 Abercrombie Street is framed
by the rectangular front window of his yellow terrace.
He is lit like a Rembrandt by his reading lamp focussed
on his workbench of small tools and small parts.

In his right eye is a black magnifying glass,
a monocle for the tiny insides of his beings.
He watches them quietly as their wheels begin to turn
clockwise and anticlockwise like the great chain of being.

For him, time is not a constant;
it moves, it has balance,
it has escapement, like life.

Without its wheels there is no fortune;
it beats on, is regular like his pulse,
now, now, now, now, now, now, now, now.

In another section called 'Tales' we encounter a range of historical and literary figures; Icarus found by two ambulance men, Macbeth, Crusoe, highly strung Ophelia and honest Laertes. Odysseus gets his own verse that beautifully highlights his qualities as a liar and a fabricator:

After a warrior
has finished killing
what do you expect
and he was handsome,
grey haired, massive arms and chest;

and later, he was in no hurry,
he enjoyed her as he might, she
having no one else for so long
and now him to herself.

She in turn loved him.

Still later he would find fault
where there was none.
He would talk insensitively of
his wife and think of home.

Much later when she had remarried
she heard a sailor tell the tale he'd heard
the great Odysseus tell
of how she had bewitched him.
('ix')

This is a very special collection, worth taking time over, and especially worth reading a second time for the subtleties and little nuances. There is a wide breadth of subject and time frame that takes us to so many past eras, and ranges widely across the globe. Definitely a book to linger over.

Marcus Hobson

Titirangi Poets

Titirangi Poets
From the Fringe of Heaven
Printable Reality, 2022
RRP $40, 132pp

The venerable group known as the Titirangi Poets has
been around since 1977. Their regular meetings in the Titirangi library were
threatened by the onset of Covid-19, which pushed them to produce 12
e-zines — electronic magazines of poetry and flash. This book is the best of
the best from those 12. To fit with the pandemic theme, the original timings
of the various lockdowns have been used as a frame, charting the ups
and downs of levels one to three, culminating in that exclusive Auckland
phenomenon, the long lockdown of August to December 2021.

The joy of such an anthology is that you never know what to
expect over the next page. That applies to quality as well as taste, but
there is something here for everyone. The sudden swing from fun
to deep reflection is an ideal way to keep readers on their toes. The
chronological frame is also a great way to remind us that initially we
took the whole lockdown experience in good humour. There were
friendly teddy bears in windows at first — 'everywhere, bubbles of
bears were isolating in windows' says John Adams in 'Bare Numbers'. By
the final lockdown all such fun feels long forgotten.

One of the gems I quickly unearthed was 'The Hidden Room' by
Richard von Sturmer. Its brief lines are worth quoting in full for the way
they expertly reveal a sense of magic.

There are a thousand rooms in the Sydney Opera House. Its
construction took fourteen years, and due to the complexity of the
design, one room was reportedly sealed up without a door. The room
became lost deep inside the building, over the decades absorbing and

storing the sounds of countless operas and concerts. If it were ever to be opened, the explosion would blow out all the windows and the whole city would be flooded with music.

My absolute favourite poem also took me to foreign shores, but in a most unexpected and provocative way. Edna Heled's 'The World Will Never Be the Same' makes us look back through history and forward through change, reminding us that few things ever stay still or remain unchanged. It also reminds us that one generation cannot always judge the feelings of another:

Germany.

To think that we can look at you
for comfort and hope
at a time
of paralyzing fear

the world will never be the same

yet Berlin is a magnet for young Israelis
Jewish descendants
third generation Holocaust
flocking to find freedom and peace
in the rebuilt hub of precedent horrors

we
children of war
should know that a world never being the same
can become a salvation

we
grandchildren of war
should know

Years ago there was a whole genre called 'nonsense verse', and I'm unsure how that has been re-christened for these more politically correct times. Robert Hoare's 'Oobus-Nimmet' is a fine example, as is his 'Pelican de Crunch'. The author's short biography says simply 'Robert was born in England in 1967. Shortly afterwards, he discovered his father's copy of *Verse and Worse*, and has never recovered.' It is likely that my enjoyment of his nonsense is down to the gift of the very same book from *my* father.

What I felt most from the collection were the interactions, the feelings for fellow human beings, collected from a time of heightened sensibility. That time when we were warned against connection. Time and again characters emerge strongly from the page. None more so than Gary, in the poem of the same name by Ashley Smith. We have lost Gary, but we are happy about the manner of his passing: 'No more hunched in your wheel-chair, / cornered in your ward trying to decrypt signals / from an increasingly besieged world.'

As it did with our thoughts about other people, lockdowns also brought into focus many simple everyday events around us. 'Making Breakfast — a love poem' by Michael Morrissey is a great example of seeing and hearing things differently:

> Through the thin wall I hear my wife chopping fruit
> as rhythmically as the piston on the steam ferry
> each sound has its own precision,
> delicate but unwavering
> surgical as the lobotomist's knife
> her kitchen blade slices apple
> cuts through pineapple
> fillets watermelon
> deals painless death to passionfruit
> a banana stands no chance
> it may sound like fruit is being cut
> but really it's the sound of love.

Not everyone enjoyed their time in lockdown, and perhaps driven insane by a shortage of reading matter, or the closed library, we hear Geoff Barlow shouting in 'Fuel for Thought':

HISTORY OF
OIL EXPLORATION
IS BLOODY BORING

Mark Prisco

James Brown

James Brown
The Tip Shop
Te Herenga Waka University Press, 2022
RRP $25, 80pp

The opening poems in James Brown's latest collection, *The Tip Shop*, feel knocked off, like when you want to get some chore over and done with because it's so tedious. We're in 'The Waiting Room', at a party talking to 'John' about nothing, and it feels like a whole lifetime; like banging a football repeatedly against the 'corrugated-iron fence' ('Mr Spencer'). Like fixing a net. Like you're picking bits off 'oblivion's final sieve' ('Collecting'), rummaging through the tip shop, flicking through those Richard Clayderman LPs and thinking 'I don't think this is what I am looking for' ('Their Feelings').

It's heavy, but the delivery is light. There's a sort of effortless not-striving-for: you know you're shit at netball ('Resilience on Checkout 7') and you just want to get over yourself and learn to laugh at your heroic failures, the vacant spaces, the missed glory. You're the butt of your own joke:

> . . . I ran into spaces
> where, if the person passing the ball had also been me, I would've
> been put through. But they weren't. Instead they turned the other
> way, beat their marker, and scored.
> ('Football Again')

What a disappointment! But James Brown is just warming up; he's re-thinking 'who I thought I was and what I thought I thought I thought' ('Flensing'); he's dismantling the giant nest, twig by twig, of dead-end suburbia, undoing the no-brainer (or is it 'hair-brained'?) schemes of housing developers (see 'Insulation'), the advisors who tell you that life is just marketing —

> ... desk-top calendar advice written by someone
> who's maybe dabbled with candles and a water feature
> ('Water Features')

— and sifting through all this takes time: 'a few days / to arrive' ('Waiheke'). He takes us down roads, empty spaces you can't remember, lonely walks back home in the drizzle where you contemplate a chance of happiness — maybe, like a kiss — not taken ('The Crystal Halo'); roads where there's a 'dog barking / at nothing to speak of, / except perhaps suburbia' ('Space and Time'); and the long wind-up panic of ghastly purple grass, the woman not breathing ('Trigger Warning').

There's a bit of fun, too ('What's Your Name?'): word games ('Focus Freya Focus'), fresh rhymes ('Agatha Panther' — which, incidentally, is my own fun name for *Agapanthus*), Winston Peters, the misplaced faith of dog owners —

> Drop it George! Drop it! *George!*
> No George! *No* George! *No!*
> He's never done that before.
> ('Dog Owners')

— and the chestnut mare farce of 'Alleged Female Orgasm', where scientific analysis collides with gravity (nature). And then, the explosion of tears and snot in 'An Explosion of Tears and Snot':

> ... Don't talk to me
> about pain until you've curled up on the clifftop.
> Don't talk to me about privilege because there is
> no silver spoon, I mean lining, I mean bullet.

Actually, that poem's less fun than a 'severed finger' ('Extended Object Label'), which *George!* the dog might know something about, and it's followed by 'Self-reflection', the penultimate poem,

> Cloudy with a chance of rain: a good day
> for a brood, so I went out into the world
> to see if someone would be mean to me,
> because there are a lot of mean people
> in the world and I would inevitably encounter one,
> and, sure enough . . .

This triggers memories of extreme hunger, of being so poor you can't afford the sugar hole of a donut, the lack of empathy. There *is* so much unkindness, which for us mostly consists of ordinary incidents, 'a small thing // that happened at the water cooler / this morning' ('Water Cooler Bubbles'), but it still hurts.

This wonderful collection of poems ends where it began — 'A Calm Day with Undulations' ('I know where / I am going / with this.') — at sea: 'Your body / afloat in salt / as if cured' ('Waiheke'). It's slow. But, like God, I like my cricket five days long — even if it does end in a draw.

Rogelio Guedea

Rogelio Guedea, translated by Roger Hickin
O me voy o te vas / One of us must go
Otago University Press, 2022
RRP $25, 81pp

These days the best poetry nearly always comes from the blandest set of circumstances, ordinary experiences like an unoiled bathroom door ('ii') or the petty irritations between couples who should have long-since parted but stay together, because they are 'helpless . . . / against love . . . ' It's a pain in the kidneys ('ii') and the heart.

Rogelio Guedea has dedicated a collection of simply numbered poems, brilliantly translated by Roger Hickin, to 'Blanca, the only country I can live in' — the woman he is condemned (it feels like a life sentence) to be with, to love. His muse, his romantic partner for 20-odd years, cops it from the opening lines of the first poem:

> You're no good at finding streets or recognising faces,
> you forget everything the moment you turn your back
> ('i')

Hardly a devastating attack, or grounds for separation. But keep reading. The domestic, low-level bitching is relentless: she is jealous (he says), ungrateful, querulous, and she has this noisy alarm clock which she never wakes to and he has to turn it off and when he complains about it she gets angry ('vii'). She drives him mad. And yet, and yet . . . he lies awake in bed looking at the moon whose light reveals her sinuous body ('xix'); during a quarrel he notices the radiance of her hair drenched in the night ('xxi'). He wants to write a poem about all this, but because she's so mad at him he has to cook his own breakfast.

But he *has* written a poem, 30 of them in fact, and from such base premises as marital over-familiarity, the poetry emerges, fluid and luminous, like a work of alchemy, a shaft of silver peering through the clouds. The obvious thing to say about these poems is that they're 'honest', 'unpretentious', and that's true. Those epithets, however, can suggest something unrefined or blunt — *telling it as it is*, which not infrequently is a substitute for good art. Guedea's poems are not merely candid, unromantic admissions; if that were the case, they would not have been worth writing (except in a text or an email); they would not even be poetry. The poetry is in how her cheeks glow in the mid-morning sun ('xi'): the beauty amidst the routine — of shopping for cucumbers and yams, or getting your hair done — the garbage and the flowers — all of which is depicted with the lightest of touches. They argue politics 'just after dinner':

> the hummingbirds had arrived to drink
> from the little fountain
> and the moon had suddenly concealed itself,
> as if it were about to rain.
> ('xiii')

The collection is about love, and the unbridgeable distance that separates one heart from another, the failure to connect, most tenderly evoked in the fifth poem where she walks in on him 'sitting in the bathroom / weeping': he listens to a song by José Luis Perales on his phone and a particular lyric stirs him up, and while he weeps he hears birds drinking water from a bowl, feels the sunlight, hears his daughter laughing in another room, and all of these incidents combine to produce a profound sense of sadness that is hard to account for. Some inexplicable feeling has seized him, and the reason for his tears cannot be explained by the facts. 'For God's sake', she says, 'shutting the door.'

> I've been looking for a street that will take me
> out of this city
> ....

you want to convince me that what's out there
is just in my imagination,
a paradise without wings,
an exotic bird the heart
can't catch hold of . . .
('xv')

This is the heart of the collection, for me. What's out there *is* in his
imagination. But also it's real — I mean *physically* real: it's no place on an
actual map, but every good poet reaches out for it like fruit off the highest
branch, whether they're conscious of it or not. Meanwhile the days keep
piling up, and it's a burden to him — all these undigested meals, one day
after another, each one indistinguishable from the next; and he is a burden
to her. Everything is connected: the 'load of days', her love — all of it ('xvii').

She becomes more remote in the later poems: by the time we get
to poem 'xxvi' her slender feet are 'dissolving in the dusk'. It's as if his
worst fear is being realised — not the fear of 'losing her / forever', but
the fear that he is 'forever / losing her' ('xxii'). There is the fear, the
consciousness of interminable oblivion, a great absence, 'like a bird /
suddenly / unable to regain the sky' ('vi'), a nostalgia —

. . . for streets that will appear when I am gone,
for women I'll never meet,
for the intimacy of trees . . .
('xxvii')

He contemplates the nightly void, the gulf between them, their wide
bed ('iv'), 'a window without a view' ('xxix'). In the end, there is an
empty blue sky, the prospect of being blotted out completely on 'an
endless lonely train, / that vanishes into infinity' ('xxx'):

I do not know if this hand that writes
your name at nightfall
will go on . . .

Mark Prisco

Tim Upperton

Tim Upperton
A Riderless Horse
Auckland University Press, 2022
RRP $24.99, 68pp

Tim Upperton's 'not finished'. Or he is 'finished', but
he's written these poems, 'a spell against death . . . Not a very good spell,
obviously' ('Mayfly'). In 'Wild Bees' we witness the poet's ineffectual
attempt to stuff the gap 'between wall and ceiling' with a tea-towel, to
shut the door against the 'lords of life', navigating the fearful menace of
wild bees zinging against your porch. There are shit picnics, fifty-third
birthdays, the deadbeat ennui of lift silence that turns killer-wild in the
imagination, for real. The anger circulates in the close atmosphere. By
the time you get out of the lift you want to punch some tall guy in the
groin. 'Calm the fuck down', declares the voice of 'Dead Pets', it's only a
fucking cat, and we can get another one.

That's easy for you to say: I loved that cat. In the end, the spade lies
on the mound, sunny-side up. You let go, because you must:

> The ground became dust
> and blew away.
> Bone remembered the flesh
> and missed its warmth,
> its softness, its weight.
>
> Bone lay white beneath the moon.
> ('Bone')

And you say sorry because you must, and that doing so, when you're a child, hurts ('YRROS'). You don't forget it. It stays with you. Even someone else's (not the poet's) memory — a doll getting snatched from your hands and smashed to the ground — feels devastating ('True Story'). The reader gets it third-hand, but it's poignant like a bee sting, time passing, a mother's song ('Nobody Knows'). 'Small Griefs' like dead thickened leaves, the emptiness of 'Lunch on the Grass', which goes wrong because you don't like potato salad, and you won't eat it, even when you're urged on by a crowd of picnickers — not even to please a woman 'very attractive to me': the poet's distracted by a tiny 'blue-green beetle of some kind' on the 'vast plane' of her thigh. 'That's the sort of day it was.' And he won't eat the potato salad. Why not? To be true to yourself? Go on, try it! For fuck's sake! Just eat it! What would you do? '[Y]ou can guess what happened next.' Whatever you do, it's going to feel shit. It's like being told to say sorry, Dick, and you don't wanna.

By the way (cough): one day you die ('Cough'). You lie in the 'wormy darkness' of your tomb, and you're lonely ('Writ on the Eve of my 53rd Birthday'). But you go on, 'writing in the dark' ('Mayflower') — for how long —

> Just as the ants in their dark troop will touch
> muzzle to muzzle — as they ask the way,
> perhaps, or how the day goes — it was such
>
> with these, who, ending their brief interplay,
> continued on their solitary paths,
> had somewhere to be, and all the day long
>
> to get through . . .
> ('roadside trees')

— (the phrasing's so slick, so Dantean!) 'How far still to go, how far' ('Roadside Trees'). It's not really a question, and you might never get there — the end — and that's even more terrifying than death. A nightmare. Like one of those you have when you're a child, and who knows where that terror comes from, and who opened the door. It's real, because it doesn't just come from nowhere. There *is* a dark world which we glimpse when we're vulnerable, when we're open. 'Homecoming'? — There is a map. There is no map: memories are dying. You say it's OK, but who knows? You are trying to inspire me with confidence, but I don't feel it. Are these people really friendly? Or are you just saying that? It's not the same anymore, is it? What you remember is undone. No one speaks of it. This doesn't feel like home.

'Welcome home' ('Homecoming'). These poems *are* a spell against death. You can inhale them when you're lying in the wormy silence. This poem, for instance:

My load, my lode,
my burden, my treasure,
you are so heavy!
How long
must I carry you?
Forever?
Very well then —
I will carry you
forever.
('Love Poem')

I love that.

Diana Bridge

Diana Bridge
Deep Colour
Otago University Press, 2023
RRP $25, 84pp

This new collection by Diana Bridge is mellifluous,
artistic and contemplative. The title poem sets out the task of the
poet: to put into words something that can only be glimpsed, like 'the
tiny floating scarf of a fin' that she barely makes out in an aquarium.
After she had completed *The Waves*, Virginia Woolf wrote that she
had 'netted that fin in the waste of water', and here Bridge shares that
impulse. Pondering the illusive fin, she asks:

> The twist of colour twirls, it comes to me
> like a lost strand in the plait of ancestry. Should I try
> and pin it down or avoid it on account of what might lie there?
> ('Deep colour')

In many of these poems she returns to the art of poetry itself. In 'Her
sort of order', she writes '*processing is my primary occupation* followed
up / by *making metaphor my next*'. Visual art and the written word fuse,
and many lines are painterly in their regard. In 'While it lived', 'Sunset
has drawn a single calligraphic line / through domes of backlit cloud
and the true blue / of the sky.' Images are precisely assigned, in the
way that the ancient Chinese poets used them, as representations of
invisible emotion. They give Bridge's poems that same allusive quality.

Her delicate and precise use of imagery is skilfully employed in
the second section, 'Utamaro's Objects'. Here ekphrasis is utilised
to wondrous effect, based on the illustrations of eighteenth-century
Japanese artist Kitagawa Utamaro. The miraculous perfection of small

orders is explored in 'Songs of the garden', where she depicts and interprets Utamaro's ink drawings from his lesser known *The Insect Book*. Lines of Utamaro's drawings are lines of poetry, 'Each reflection is quickened by a likeness', and opportunities abound for comparison to human experience: 'Those who sat / on riverbanks shuffling their sly, erotic, night-time topics'. By focusing her acute, poetic eye on the smallest and most delicate, Bridge has selected for her art a micro world that reveals the most telling aspects of human nature. I adored 'bagworm and scarb', in which the 'minomushi' or bagworm's 'self-woven houses' are compared to 'a chandelier that drops in icicles from its host tree'. '[T]hey gather and merge' contains the most touching portrayal of love, where a grasshopper 'stretches out towards his love the reins of his small heart'.

Bridge's poetry is enriching and reflects also her love and knowledge of classical Chinese poetry. Her sensitive lines arrive perfectly weighted, simple and surprising. This is life close up. In the third section, 'Fifteen Poems on Things: Translations', Bridge's versions of the poems of fifth-century poet Xie Tiao become their own remarkable pieces. Her contemporary cadences hold the original images aloft in the air, as the poem 'the bamboo' exhibits delightfully:

In the moonlight leaves sparse-etched then dense;
In the breeze it stretches up, then bends again

The power of images in ancient Chinese poetry to communicate deep-felt emotion and abstract concepts comes through impeccably in these versions. Connections are everywhere, culminating in the fourth section of this collection, in which Bridge returns to a poetry of transformation. Transcendence is hinted at throughout, indeed it's mentioned explicitly in 'The flying creatures' and explored in 'Here comes my soul'. All things great and small feature in this soulful, elegant collection, alive with symbolism, and like the 'creatures caught on the wing / before they can transform, mutate or age', the poems of *Deep Colour* capture life in its moments of becoming.

Elizabeth Smither

Elizabeth Smither
My American Chair
Auckland University Press, 2022
RRP $24.99, 88pp

This is one of the most delightful books of poetry I've read for some time. Smither is a master of all forms, and the deeply felt and eager appreciation of human life in this latest collection is a treat indeed. This is a book to cherish, one that offers solace and warmth as Smither celebrates life with an appreciation of the quiet power of humour.

I laughed aloud at the playfulness of 'The joke of the Sapeur-Pompiers' and 'Poem for the Hippocratic Society about the brain: *Lambs brains in white sauce*'. Frivolity is exalted with a heartening optimism in poems like 'The Whistle dress', and we can indulge in the sumptuousness of the 'fine Egyptian sheets 500 threads' in 'Fine Egyptian sheets'. Smither's curiosity about life's best things is a driving force, and experiences and observations are beautifully expressed with understated elegance: 'The way / apples seem to hide, as if / the surrounding leaves like a duenna // hold green shade in front of blushing skin.' These poems embrace an unexpected happiness in ordinary things and moments.

Even the more serious moments are inflected with a *joie de vivre* — 'I check the profile of the cardiologist I am seeing. / His hobbies: wine, women, song, bush, wild animals' ('Animal blouses') — and optimism radiates from the refrain '*The heart heals itself between beats*' in 'Poem for the Hippocratic Society about the heart'. Many poems arrive like moments prised open, turned and regarded, and then generously shared. Sounds are relished and adored in lines such as 'white lies like butterflies', and 'a lamp shaped like a pantaloon'. Smither rejoices in their reverberations: 'I still say *gentile* to myself when I dust / the little white porcelain jardinière.'

Surprising moments gleam throughout: 'It is words, you clowns, the other laureate thinks / not sun in her eyes', and names ring out and are pitched like souvenirs. Compelling encounters are lit by the commodious and touching tone with which Smither brings us on adventures in the ordinary. I found myself scouring the pages for a poem that returned to me unexpectedly (it was the exquisite 'At Sainte-Chapelle').

Pleasure, gratitude and contentment merge in splendidly informal lines such as in 'Eating ice cream in the historic house', in which the scoops are 'vaudeville colours / or chocolate and rum and raisin'. However, sophisticated syntax lingers long after reading, demonstrating Smither's lifelong devotion to the art of poetry:

> [. . .] Listening and waiting
> is for angels their daily bread: a glass
>
> wafer that slides down the throat
> and disappears under their glassy gowns.
> ('Angels')

She returns to femininity and the maternal, her fine gift for poetic anecdote on display, in 'The white lilies', which compares flowers to 'fifteen girls who have changed into / white debutante dresses or five women / who have danced all night and come home with the milkman', and in the strange and dreamlike 'The man who wanted to stroke my hair'. Childhood and memory bring forth inspired lines in 'The Swan Neck', 'Two pregnant daughters-in-law' and 'Night-time words to Ruby'. I loved their tenderness, particularly in the last, where Smither intones:

> Beautiful girl, beautiful girl in your tower
> not far from the ceiling which you could reach.
> I am bringing something I do not know

down to you in my embrace. An angel's
wingtip, the first air movement of

a visitation of coming and forever grace.
Beautiful girl, beautiful girl.
('Night-time words to Ruby')

Smither's lines are filled with a gorgeous vivacity. A buoyancy prevails.
Their intimacy brings sheer pleasure. Her American writing chair of
the title poem must be farewelled, but this collection shows a craft that
continues to thrive in sumptuous poems, reminders of the delightful
and forward-looking side of New Zealand verse in which 'cherry trees /
signal like fairylights and declaim their liturgy / *Hope, hope, hope* along
the edges.' When I read this collection, it was what I most needed.

Stephanie de Montalk

Stephanie de Montalk
As the trees have grown
Te Herenga Waka University Press, 2023
RRP $25, 104pp

The strength and fragility of trees are perfect analogies for the wisdom Stephanie de Montalk shares in *As the trees have grown*. This is a deeply meditative book, yet alive with the grit, resolve and light humour necessary for survival in the human body. A life force flows through these thought-provoking poems as de Montalk probes mysteries of growth and decay with the lightest touch, elevating the ordinary to the marvellous.

A fresh and airy effect is delivered by two-line stanzas, often of just one or two words. Some seem to end mid-flight, leaving the reader suspended with the poem. Trees throw light on life's mysteries, bringing the poet to a height from which the world can be surveyed and endlessly rediscovered in metaphorical play. In 'Imperium', a conifer's 'habit / of dancing while rocking // itself into a dream / invited orchestration' — just one version of her own stories.

De Montalk's refined and moving poetic view looks impermanence right in the eye, contemplating with a philosopher's gaze 'the scent // of a twig / petrified forever // in a gap between opening and closing'. There are beautiful lines like 'the glabrous shade // of the laurel bay' and 'All day there was / a deep white light // and everything / with an edge to it'. Travel poems such as 'Trance' and 'In Passing' allow de Montalk scope for awe and wonder, and for displaying her delicate appreciation of trees and birdlife. Here, the natural world is a guide, associate and friend.

A playfulness binds many of these poems. 'ASA 400', 'Decoction of Futurism' and 'Park Life' display interlocking sounds, rhythm and humour: 'Futurist strips of cirrus // wrestling themselves / into trousers —' and 'The Blues groom // themselves / and wave their tails, // paw pads cool / and clover damp, // cobby bodies / and amber eyes'. Intensely wrought poems like 'Heartfelt' and 'Time-distant' give way to lighter reflections that convey the healing power of nature. The names of trees, flowers and birds are dropped into small, clipped lines like a rollcall of friends, their names radiating preciousness.

As though moving in full circle, the final section returns to a meditation on life, corporeality and daily offerings. There is always hope in these poems, like the 'newly grafted / branchlings // on light-starved elms / at the heart // of the forest / where the foliage // is pale and thin, / but the going is easy'. A fluid movement of sound propels the final poem of this collection, in which peace is drawn from slowing down and inhabiting, through sleep or perhaps in poetic dream, the slipstream of life:

no recall
of the comforting,

softly plausible rhythms
of rain,

sun and wind
at dawn

after the balm
of sleep

has untangled
and knitted up

the stressed yarns
of the sleave of care
('A Sleave of Care')

De Montalk's poems, some previously published and gathered together here alongside new works, exhibit a beautiful and philosophical celebration of imagination, while the world around is memorialised in its rush for bloom and survival.

Michelle Rahurahu

Ruby Solly

Ruby Solly
The Artist
Te Herenga Waka University Press, 2023
RRP $30, 144pp

Mō tātou, ā, mō kā uri, ā muri ake nei

I have to admit Ruby is a bro of mine. Aotearoa is small enough; the Maaori kuumara vine is smaller. What I might be able to offer in way of a review is an insight into the author as a person and how that personality permeates the puuraakau. Ruby is a ringatoi who uses as many tools to create as she can find. She is a musician, an arts therapist, a writer and a poet. She paints, she sings, she mimics celebrities and animals like a parrot, she plays the wind as well as she plays the cello. A common afternoon with Ruby can be spent sitting in her whare and, after an hour, she will drop a curious contraption into your lap without comment. She has a patupaiarehe-like ability to make you forget you are self-conscious so you can try something new. She is an Artist.

I read earlier versions of this manuscript, and was a small voice commenting on it before the public did. But I can't claim much of an influence, because everything inside the verse novel *The Artist* is uniquely Ruby's, and, through Ruby, uniquely Kaai Tahu, Kaati Maamoe, Waitaha. It harkens a new revival of specificity in Maaori writing, not so fixated with the clear delineation of what Maaoritanga is next to the wider Paakehaa world, but the delineation between iwi of the north and south. And the story of that stark identity in the south is so maunga-steady; it is a song that is sung regardless of whether there are ears to hear it.

The narrative is split into five sections of accounts touching on three distinct generations, which are displayed visually in an arrangement of 'Kā Kaitapere' cards at each section. This is translated as 'players' in the text, named like the thespians in Shakespearean theatre and, in my mind, captures the diversity of their performance; they can operate as any role in a story — as dramatic actors, as clowns, as musicians. It is reminiscent of essa may ranapiri's *Echidna*, which begins with a dramatis personae, indicating a bit of mischief, a bit of play. These are both writers who would be discontented with a straightforward telling of a story — they require room to explore.

I've heard some koorero on the cards; Ruby painted them herself, and they originally served as tactile moving parts she could shift around as she wrote. I think, for a reader, they also serve as references to the tuupuna peering out from the page, the same way our tuupuna peer down from the mantel in many of our whare.

To listen to taangata Maaori speak of themselves, you must sift through a good 20 generations or so. These are tall tales. To be Indigenous is to be a singular strand woven over hundreds of others. It's only natural that to tell a singular story there be many starts and many endings, and for many of those starts and ends to be twisted around themselves and strung together. I have sat at the feet of many friends, whaanau and experts, listening to such recitations as they gestured to paintings or carvings of tuupuna, and have felt a sense of meditative stillness. Time passes and yet I am fixed, woven into the surroundings. I have a sense of direction, I have landmarks. Here is the whare, here are the tuupuna, open the door and see all ngaa tuhanga.

The first section, 'Kōrero Tuatahi', guides the reader through the histories of Kaai Tahu, Kaati Maamoe, Waitaha, through the complexities and violence of Aotearoa. A particular favourite of mine is 'Whawhai', which recounts the Ngaati Toa attack on Kaiapoi Paa during the Musket Wars:

At first these are plentiful times:
food swings across the river
    Kai-a-poi, Kai-a-poi,

Until the song brings itself forward again
In the sound of raupō in the wind.
                    Hide the children, hide the children.
Some hear the song and listen,
But sadly other lines will be cut.
Families to become blunt hei toki,
No longer shaping the world.

Then the men come.

There is talk of stolen stone,
of moko slipping from the face.
Tools of the white man's war
ring out,
like stones
dropping
from the skies.

The feeling of tau increases as each verse stacks together the three components of southern whakapapa and enters the next section, 'Kōrero Tuarua'. Perhaps it was the quality of the words arranged in verse, or the dreamlike way the narrative glides from history to history. Or perhaps it's the music that resounds through the narratives, acting as a backing track that can be lifted in the mix of the story at the right times, then faded into the background. It never recedes entirely, but it transforms from sound to a physical object into a place. I feel as I read I am being taught how to listen intently.

He is captured.
Not by foreign enemy
or the white men,
but by a song
spiralling out
from the source.

He wakes with the koukou
of the ruru.
Feels the rope of the song
around him
in all the parts
that can't be seen.
He moves through the bush
With moonlight to guide him.
       A slow walk at first
       Then the rope tightens
          And he is running
          Towards *the raki,*
          Towards *the song.*
(Whaiāipo)

Anchored in history, we move forward into the next generation. The sections 'Kōrero Tuarua' and 'Kōrero Tuatoru' focus on the main characters of the narrative: maamaa and paapaa, Hana and Matiu, and the twins, Te Heikiki and Reremai. The resonance of te taiao hits a new frequency as the story heralds in children through these two sections: even before the twins are born, the music is emanating through the story.

'Kōrero Tuatoru' is where the calabash-breakers of the narrative erupt into the story and break up the strict verse format of the earlier sections. This is where we see an inclusion of a piece written as an italicised scene script between the parents, mirrored by a similar scene between the two rangatahi in their own bedroom. It is also a relaxing of the highly poetic style, as the section is all dialogue, and yet the presentation tells us that this is still a part of the fiction of the story.

These are players, reading their lines, in the scene of 'The Bedrooms'. In this way, I am hesitant to take the conversations as genuine, but rather as a construction built on the unvoiced fears of each character that are known and felt between each of them:

Scene: The Bedroom of Matiu and Hana

Scene: The Bedroom of Te Heikiki and Reremai

H: But Kiki can't be married — how will she ask for help if she can't speak? She should stay with me.

R: I want to be a carver, Kiki.

M: She has a better chance than Rere — they can't even see the stone they worship so much. Rere'll be sitting at that workbench touching those bloody stones until you put me in the ground.

K: They'll never allow it. It's too dangerous. I know how the stone feels to you — it's like me when I'm dancing. It's like a marriage between you and the stone.

Without spoiling some key events in the last sections, 'Kōrero Tuawhā' is a powerful account of a period of darkness that breaks through the predispositions that the whaanau holds for the twins, and in doing so enables a cathartic release from pain — 'Kōrero Whakanoa', a period of celebration after a challenging time. What the artist expresses best is the ways in which learning about new ways of doing is best achieved by learning the language that comes from an alternative perspective: the language of the wind and skies, the language of stone, the language of the land. Reremai and Te Heikiki are an example of living ancestors who exemplify the Maaori way of communicating, which is simply: whatever is most natural with whatever tools the land provides.

This is a koorero that challenges and delights on the first read and the thousandth read. A true taonga that adds to a proud and long set of puuraakau for southern iwi, and a pounamu-green koha for Maaori iwi at large. Kia kaha ngaa koorero tangata whenua!

Naveena Menon

Jane Arthur

Jane Arthur
Calamities!
Te Herenga Waka University Press, 2023
RRP $25, 72pp

'I want to get morbid I want to get morbid' Arthur begins in her poem 'How, All Right' — and she does. The unsettling rises to the surface of her collection like an oil slick, darkly iridescent, and with each poem I found myself wading deeper despite the burn.

Calamities! is split into three sections: 'Risk Assessment', 'The Bear', and 'Highly Flammable'. In 'Risk Assessment', Arthur paints an eerily memetic picture of a simmering apocalypse. Unlike Hollywood's usual portrayals of The End — sudden and all at once — we face an extinction 'kind of like / getting cooked alive but so slowly you'll / probably barely notice it'. She acutely captures the emotional dissonance of living in our uncertain times, staring down the barrel of climate change while living in a global pandemic and watching as princes, priests and people in power do things they shouldn't.

It's never been easier to take stock of our world and keep informed (despite the 'disinformation activists'' best efforts) and yet 'the more one learns, the worse one feels!' Sometimes, it's easier to wish we lived somewhere with cupboards so we wouldn't have to see the flies dying in our cups, to 'find an absent middle-distance and aim for it'. Nevertheless, 'Risk Assessment' manages to push back against fatalism even as it grapples with a looming, ever-present anxiety and the numbness that arises from it:

I'm tired of
picking and choosing
pain that sits nicely

like a kid on the mat
who's bleeding internally
('What Has Changed')

In 'The Bear', we watch through the eyes of a helpless narrator as a
once towering, fiery bear is reduced to skin hanging loose around a
shrunken, unwaking body. 'The Bear' is stylistically different from the
two sections that bookend it. It is a longer-form poem and although
each stanza is only a couple of lines long, taking up less than half a
page's space, Arthur manages to infuse each with startling physical
detail and emotional resonance: goats with blank, keyhole eyes stare
out from among pursed-lipped daffodils. The white space after each
stanza reads like a release of breath, moments of silence paid in respect
to a magnificent creature's dying.

Each stanza is also punctuated by two forward slashes (//) which
appear to mark the impassive passage of time and give the impression
of a slowing heartbeat. The final stanza, however, ends with three
slashes (///), calling to mind a tally with all its finality and unsettling
implications. Here, Arthur uses the white space to cement the weight of
resigned impotence hanging over each stanza.

Finally, in 'Highly Flammable', Arthur cups her hands around the
embers of the bear's warmth and blows. As the title suggests, the poems
in 'Highly Flammable' crackle with stubborn resilience, quiet intimacy
and a wry appreciation for the messiness of living. Arthur's deft
deployment of humour does not detract from her message but rather
gives it additional depth — much like 'a silly old friend who doesn't
make life easier / but at least makes it fuller somehow'.

Arthur coaxes our attention to small moments of peace in 'the
glow / of evening sun across the branches / of trees that refuse to be
anything but green', allowing us to dig our little holes and make our
days a bit more manageable. 'Highly Flammable' reveals that, despite
our bumbling search for 'the manual for living', we scuttle about like
cockroaches 'bad at dying, good at inuring', doing okay, really, all things
considered.

Calamities! is a thought-provoking body of work that speaks to the transience of hope in our current times. However, Arthur also shows us that 'while we're looking, there remains the possibility of something better'.

What is the alternative?
Always, always a life
Without cruelty.
('Princes and Priests')

Morgan Bach

Morgan Bach
Middle Youth
Te Herenga Waka University Press, 2023
RRP $25, 96pp

Every so often, if we're lucky, a book finds its way to us and alters us at an atomic level, consuming us as much as we consume it. Morgan Bach's *Middle Youth* is one such book for me; it 'coats me as I coat it with old cells, leaves me richer and emptier'. Unrepentantly bitter with an excess of teeth, Bach wades through a present of inherited mess, the past a heat haze overlay weighting our days, and looks into the black hole of future — 'the space / outside that thin layer enclosing life' — with unflinching vulnerability and pointed fury.

> the violence done to the minds
> and bodies of our mothers,
> before our time, works like a glacier
> moving slowly on our selves
> ('carousel')

The poems in *Middle Youth* have a slippery, sensuous quality that blurs the edges of things. Boundaries between person, place, and time are more diffuse: 'What is a self but a place / to journey outwards from?' Particles evaporate, desiccating skin becomes dust lining our shelves, becomes embodied in the outdoors like so many ghosts of the earth, from dinosaurs to colonial histories. Time keeps spilling into elsewhere, 'the minutes call its past tense into existence', and the middle youth of adulthood stretches out and disappears behind us though we're still dewy. Throughout there is a real sense of tension between the fragility of life and a gaping future, the push and pull of walking through the world with our grandmother's hair, wondering if it'll lose its colour before we're swallowed, and trying to be okay about it, to 'feel lucky it's happening at all'.

'Framing is everything' 'is the paint on my nails, turning feet from slugs / to sirens'. Women deemed past their 'peak' are put 'out to pasture in the minds of men, who in all our lifetimes / have been the ones to decide'. Plagues and ecological crises are dismissed by great men drunk on figures, watching us burn in our tangle of fairy-lit, late-stage capitalism.

Middle Youth is an emphatic 'fuck you' to this tradition of great men. Bach writes our fears with cosmic weight and dares to imagine, to open herself to diffusion. She finds the energy it takes to be a person in an intimate relationship with nature, looks 'for balance to the red interiors / in a calm sea of grasses', in 'small facts / of affection, tokens of the world, ideas that prove / your love of it and, by extension, me'. Her settings are lush and textural, ripe with scent-memories and warm to the touch. I certainly believe her when she says, 'No one has ever / loved you like / a location'. *Middle Youth* is full of startling imagery that lingers long after the last page:

> The theoretical heart, size of a sweet mango, cradled in me —
> it helped to think of it as abstract, folded away by a repetition
> of men, a little drier each time, good with citrus
> and chilli, growing sharp.
> ('Pluto')

Middle Youth is an exciting follow-up to Bach's debut collection *Some of Us Eat the Seeds*, and every bit as devouring. She is a writer through whose skin I want to keep experiencing the world.

Sudha Rao

Sudha Rao
On elephant's shoulders
The Cuba Press, 2022
RRP $25, 82pp

On elephant's shoulders is a dance given form on the page. Rao's words shimmer with movement and sure-footed grace, and I found myself buoyed by her current of memories from the Indian Ocean to the Pacific.

The poems in *On elephant's shoulders* explore identity and inheritance, particularly their inextricability from place. Rao does this by transforming each moment, however small or seemingly mundane, into a sensory 'miasma of minutiae' as bold and intricate as the embroidered elephant on the book's cover. In this collection the natural world is a character in its own right, and there are recurring symbols of birds (swallows and tūī), blue oceans and braided rivers, rain and wind, ngaio and pōhutukawa, mountain ridge and whispering seeds. Indeed, each poem is strongly rooted in a sense of place and space, toes digging into new soil and overhead a kōwhai blooming 'proudly golden'.

Combined with Rao's instinctive feel for rhythm, this imbues the collection with a pulse — the ebb and flow of coastlines, the drag of a comb through hair, 'the sun's turning' 'in the journey of every swallow', and a 'salty foam mark ankled like a beating heart'. There is a real physicality to her writing, a 'grandmother's tapping, tapping the geography of her' — both the poet's identity and the textual body is in a state of flux, 'leaning into reflection of being'. The result is a reflexive meandering, a careful unpicking and re-stitching of self and relatedness — to heritage, gender, land, water bodies, and Othered brown bodies.

Rao often uses first and second person address, weaving us right up against a 'scooped grain of memory', yet even when she uses third person we are drawn right into the 'flotsam of hair, cries, screws, metal, luggaged memories, sighs, prayer and closed eyes'. Her textural details feather the pages. As a fellow South Asian Hindu living in Aotearoa, I felt my fingers smudge sense-memory grease from 'cotton wicks in oil cupped in a brass lamp' with each turn of the page. My eyes would latch onto the procession of her words teeming like ants 'bound for a crack in the wall' — through Rao's keen eye, marginal and liminal spaces (migrant, pupa, Other) are given vivid relief.

Rao begins her remarkable collection with 'Warp and weft', a poem split into three sections: 'Passages', 'Shadows', and 'Braids'. This title alone sets the tone of this tapestry of interconnectedness. Familial threads formed of 'muscle and bones' and 'veins so daring they bulge blue braids' extend across waters, longing made manifest around a wrist as a 'bracelet of memories bearing the weight' of absence and gestures forgotten. Mythology tethers past and present through black tresses and black stone tablets, inky like the 'shadow of a flame with wings', its embers crackling bright in Rao's work.

With 'Warp and weft' as the exception, Rao weaves Sanskrit terms throughout the first half of her collection, and te reo Māori and Tongan words in the second half, a metatextual parallel to her migrant experience, showcasing her as a product of her South Indian roots transplanted into Pacific soil. Her poetry is all the more sonically rich because of this, demonstrating the centrality of a mother's tongue in shaping our voices, as well as how language can function as a bridge to understanding.

> syllables
> sable, able, label,
> a howl
> is not an abyss
> if it is yell —
> bless
> ('Lament')

I've read this collection over and over again since it found its way into my hands, and I notice something new each time. There is longing and pain, but *On elephant's shoulders* is also a 'map of all [the poet's] content'. Rao is clearly a writer comfortable in the ambiguities of experience.

Khadro Mohamed

Khadro Mohamed
We're All Made of Lightning
We Are Babies (now Tender Press), 2022
RRP $25, 91pp

We're All Made of Lightning is the first published book of poetry by Wellington poet Khadro Mohamed and was the recipient of the 2023 Jessie Mackay Prize for Best First Book of Poetry. The collection gracefully tackles themes of displacement, racism and grief through striking imagery.

The reader is immediately drawn to the incredible front cover, which features a baobab tree with a tūī perched upon its root-like branches. At the foot of the tree is a silhouette of a girl whose headscarf is being blown by a night wind. The title is printed in bold yellow, like lightning cutting through the otherwise dark cover. So much of Mohamed's identity is revealed by the three pictorial elements on the cover before we even come to read the words on the pages within: her identity as a Somalian, a Muslim woman and a New Zealander.

The book is in four parts, each beginning with a chapter page that includes illustrations of distinctive New Zealand native plants, opposite a single letter from the Arabic language. Much as she has done with the book's cover, Mohamed has placed two symbols of her identity in close proximity. The Arabic letters on the first page are explained on the subsequent page, a kind of lesson and a puzzle-piece to take along to the end of the book. The poems in 'Part One' take the reader on a journey alongside the poet; we feel as though we are strangers in a foreign land, clinging to the words on the page for a sense of security. Through the use of visceral imagery we are host to the poet's sense of displacement and the urge to seek familiarity.

At the beginning of the book the reader follows the unidentified 'I' through their travels in Cairo, where they are confronted by a taxi driver who presents the first direct line of dialogue. *'You Somali?'* ('The First Time') sits on its own and in italics, a jarring interruption to the flow of the majority of the text on the page. It takes the reader aback, like an interrogation.

The flow is re-established when the taxi driver begins to try to connect with the narrator by telling her that he is familiar with her home country and has visited it himself. 'He laughs then, like it's all a funny joke'. This places the reader on guard yet again, as Mohamed evokes a sense of unease, isolation and desperation:

> I resist the urge to cut my palm wide open, to watch the skin bleed, to press my ear against the crimson and listen to it rush, desperate to hear something familiar

In 'Part Two', Mohamed leads the reader through the grief of the 15 March terror attacks in Christchurch. She describes a feeling of betrayal and the fear that the attacks could spark more violence, an anxiety many Muslims in Aotearoa felt, just as they felt unable to express their rage and pain when offered sympathy.

> All I could do was nod and say, *Thank you,* because I didn't want her to take me under
> ('On March 15')

We're All Made of Lightning takes the reader through many worlds, across coarse and rocky terrain, under spring rain and over cardamom hills. Pack your bags and let us all meet at 'The Beginning'.

Contributors

Abigail Marshall writes from a little rented room in Kirikiriroa Hamilton. You can read her poems and short stories in *Landfall, Poetry Aotearoa Yearbook, Mayhem* and *Flash Frontier*. She is working on her first novel as part of a Master of Professional Writing at the University of Waikato Te Whare Wānanga o Waikato.

Adrienne Jansen writes fiction and non-fiction, but poetry is her first love. She has published four collections, and her poems have been reproduced in several publications and anthologies. She is the co-founder of small Wellington publisher Landing Press, which specialises in poetry with a social edge that many people can enjoy. She lives in Tītahi Bay, north of Wellington.

Aimee-Jane Anderson-O'Connor was the featured poet in *Poetry New Zealand Yearbook 2021*. Her work has appeared in *Starling, Mayhem, Brief, Poetry Aotearoa Yearbook, Landfall, Turbine | Kapohau, Mimicry, Minarets, Sweet Mammalian, Sport* and *Verge, The Journal of Commonwealth Literature* and, most recently, *No Other Place to Stand: An Anthology of Climate Change Poetry from Aotearoa New Zealand* (Auckland University Press, 2022). She is a keen zine-ster and collage-maker, and believes in the power of community and collaboration.

alana hooton is a North Shore resident, university student and long-time lover and writer of poetry; her favourite poet and biggest inspiration is her grandma, Alice Hooton. In her spare time, she listens to hours of vinyl records and dreams of living on a Greek island.

Alex Nolan is an event planner who lives in Wellington. She studied creative writing at Victoria University's International Institute of Modern Letters. After a long hiatus from writing, she became a māmā in 2020, which reignited the spark. Her writing is an attempt to find original words for her parenting journey when every cliché about how wonderful and difficult it is is true.

Alice Hooton lives in Mairangi Bay Tāmaki Makaurau Auckland. Her work has been published in New Zealand and overseas.

Amanda Joshua's work has been published in *Starling, takahē, London Grip* and the *Poetry Aotearoa Yearbook*. She is a big fan of Mary Oliver, crisp mornings and phoning her mum at every minor inconvenience.

Amaris Janel Henderson is a singer-songwriter and poet who lives in Nashville, Tennessee. Her debut chapbook, *Spread*, was published by Bottlecap Press in 2023. That same year, she released two singles: 'Lemon, Lime & Bitters' and 'Undead' under her stage name Amaris. Outside of music and poetry, Amaris enjoys spending time with her New Zealand husband, Luke.

Amber Abbott is a prose writer, poet and occasional academic who is completing their Master of Professional Writing at the University of Waikato Te Whare Wānanga o Waikato.

Amber Sadgrove is a Brighton-born feminist poet who lives in Kirikiriroa Hamilton. In 2015, she graduated from the Guildford School of Acting in the United Kingdom and became part of the London poetry scene. After moving back to Aotearoa New Zealand, Amber completed a Bachelor of Arts in writing studies and then a Master of Professional Writing at the University of Waikato Te Whare Wānanga o Waikato. Her work has been published in the *Poetry Aotearoa Yearbook* and *sour cherry mag.*

Anna Jackson-Scott writes short stories, essays and poetry, and lives in Tāmaki Makaurau Auckland. Her work has appeared in *More Than a Roof* (Landing Press, 2021), *Everything I Know About Books* (Whitireia Publishing, 2023), on The Spinoff's Friday Poem and in *Womankind* magazine.

Anthony Kohere (Ngāti Porou, Rongowhakaata, Muaūpoko, Waikato-Tainui, Ngāti Tūwharetoa) is a writer and experimental filmmaker. Anthony's poems have appeared in *Mayhem* and *Poetry Aotearoa Yearbook*, and his abstract short films have been selected for the Experimental Film Festival, the Māoriland Film Festival and the Wairoa Māori Film Festival.

Anuja Mitra lives in Tāmaki Makaurau Auckland. Her poetry has been published in *Landfall, takahē* and, most recently, *Haven Speculative*. In her spare time, she enjoys patting her cats and spending too much time in indie bookstores.

Anushka Dissanayake is a year 11 student at Epsom Girls Grammar School in Tāmaki Makaurau Auckland. Her poem 'just a teen' won first prize in the 2023 *Poetry Aotearoa Yearbook* student poetry competition.

Ben Jardine is a New Zealand-American writer, poet and performer. His fiction has been shortlisted in the 2021 and 2022 National Flash Fiction Day competition and been published in *Flash Frontier*. His poetry appeared in *Poetry New Zealand Yearbook 2022*.

Brent Cantwell is from Tīmaru and lives with his family in the Gold Coast hinterland in Australia. His work has recently been published in *Meniscus, Poetry Aotearoa Yearbook* and *Mayhem*. His first collection, *tether*, was published by Recent Work Press in 2023.

Brent Kininmont's poetry can be found in a range of places, including in the *Poetry Aotearoa Yearbook* and *Ōrongohau | Best New Zealand Poems,* and in his collection *Thuds Underneath* (Te Herenga Waka University Press, 2016).

Britt Clark is an actor/writer type who is originally from the Waikato. She lives in Tāmaki Makaurau Auckland and is studying for a master's in creative writing at Massey University. She spends her time working as a sketch comedy writer.

Bronte Heron is a poet and educator who was born in Hāwera and lives in New York City. They are a Master of Fine Arts candidate at The New School and a graduate of the International Institute of Modern Letters. Their work has been published by platforms such as the *Baltimore Review, Landfall, takahē, Turbine | Kapohau,* The Spinoff and *Mayhem.* They are a Fulbright scholar, a literacy tutor, a dog-walker, a community organiser, a vendor at the Fort Greene Park farmers market, a loiterer and a fierce friend.

Carin Smeaton lives in Tāmaki Makaurau Auckland with her whānau. She works at a central city research library. She studies a bit and writes a bit more. Recently she's been published in *Te Awa o Kupu* (Penguin Random House, 2023).

Charles Ross is a year 12 student who lives next to a tidal estuary in Waitati, just outside Ōtepoti Dunedin. His poem 'Hikaroroa' won first prize in the 2023 *Poetry Aotearoa Yearbook* student poetry competition.

Chris Stewart lives in Ōtautahi Christchurch. His poems have been published in a range of New Zealand journals, including *Landfall* and *Sweet Mammalian,* and previously in the *Poetry Aotearoa Yearbook.* A selection of his work was featured in *AUP New Poets 6.*

Chrys Anthemum is a Waikato-based artist and performer. She is creatively nomadic, refusing to settle on any one medium, and uses her crafts to navigate the world as a queer, chronically ill person. Her previous poetic forays can be found in *Mayhem* or online at *Free the Verse.*

Cindy Botha lives in Tauranga. Her poems have appeared in magazines and anthologies in the United Kingdom, the United States, Australia and Aotearoa New Zealand.

Cindy Zeiher teaches modernist and postmodernist theories in the human services programme at the University of Canterbury Te Whare Wānanga o Waitaha. She plays the cello and writes poetry about the subjective experience of being caught within language(s).

Clare Riddell is a poet who lives in Kemureti Cambridge, Aotearoa New Zealand. Her work has been published in *sour cherry mag, Poetry Aotearoa Yearbook* and *Mayhem.*

Dadon Rowell is a poet and short fiction writer who lives in Kirikiriroa Hamilton. She's a teacher and librarian. Her work has featured in multiple journals and anthologies and most recently she guest co-edited the tenth issue of *Mayhem*.

David Čiurlionis is a poet and prose writer who works in Te Wao Nui a Tiriwa the Waitākere Ranges. His work has been featured in *Poetry Aotearoa Yearbook*, *Mayhem* and on Newsroom, and in the UK collection *Radgepacket — Tales from the Inner City*. He has a master's degree in creative writing from the Waipapa Taumata Rau University of Auckland.

David Simes was born in Essex, grew up in Tauranga, studied in Kirikiriroa Hamilton, and now lives in Wellington, where he is studying for a PhD in theatre and comics. His essay 'Mr Fox and Me' was highly commended in *Landfall*'s 2020 Charles Brasch Young Writers' Essay Competition. His poetry has been published in *Mayhem*, and his academic work has been published by *The Journal of Commonwealth Literature* and Palgrave Macmillan.

David Wrigley is a writer and musician from Kemureti Cambridge who lives with his partner and two sons beneath the long shadow of Mount Nittany in Central Pennsylvania. He is applying the finishing touches to his first novel, *Ghost Town*, waiting for the leaves to change and making do with a child's ukulele.

Devon Webb is a poet and writer who lives in Aotearoa New Zealand. She writes full-time, exploring themes of femininity, sexuality, youth and vulnerability, and shares her poetry online and through live performance. Her work has been widely published both locally and internationally, including on The Spinoff, *The Big Idea*, *Salient, a fine line, bad apple* and *Rat World*. She is the two-time Wellington Slam Poetry Champion, and is editing her debut novel, *The Acid Mile*.

Eliana Gray is a poet who lives in Ōtepoti Dunedin. You can find their work in places such as *Landfall, Cordite Poetry Review*, The Spinoff and *Mayhem*.

Elizabeth Morton is a yarn-teller and neuroscience enthusiast from Tāmaki Makaurau Auckland. Her latest collection of poetry is *Naming the Beasts* (Otago University Press, 2022).

Elliot McKenzie (they/them) is a poet who lives in Tāmaki Makaurau Auckland. Their poems have previously been published in *Starling, Tarot, Sweet Mammalian* and *Ōrongohau | Best New Zealand Poems*.

Erena Shingade (Pākehā) lives in Tāmaki Makaurau Auckland. She works as an editor and book publicist and is a graduate of India's Seagull School of Publishing.

Her writing has been included in places such as *Art + Australia, International Gallerie,* RM Gallery, *Landfall* and on The Spinoff, and she co-edited *Past the Tower, Under the Tree: Twelve Stories of Learning in Community* (Gloria Books, 2023).

Erik Kennedy (he/him) is the author of the poetry collections *Another Beautiful Day Indoors* (2022) and *There's No Place Like the Internet in Springtime* (2018), both with Te Herenga Waka University Press, and he co-edited *No Other Place to Stand,* a book of climate change poetry from Aotearoa and the Pacific (Auckland University Press, 2022). He lives in Ōtautahi Christchurch.

essa may ranapiri (Waikato-Tainui, Ngaati Raukawa, Te Arawa, Ngaati Puukeko, Clan Gunn, Horwood) is a person who lives on Ngaati Wairere whenua. They are the author of *ransack* (2019) and *Echidna* (2022), both with Te Herenga Waka University Press, and a PhD student looking at how poetry by taangata takataapui engages with atuatanga. They co-edited *Kupu Toi Takataapui | Takataapui Literary Journal* with Michelle Rahurahu. They have a great love for language, Land Back and hot chips. They will write until they're dead.

Ethan Christensen (he/him) is a writer from the Coromandel who is studying towards a writing studies degree at the University of Waikato Te Whare Wānanga o Waikato. His work has been published on The Spinoff, in *Mayhem, Overcommunicate, sour cherry mag* and others. He has a keen interest in photography, and hopes others can see themselves in the lived experiences he puts to the page.

Evie Howell is completing a master's in professional writing at the University of Waikato Te Whare Wānanga o Waikato.

Frances Libeau is a writer and sonic artist from Tāmaki Makaurau Auckland. Their writing has been published or placed and won awards with *Overland* (Australia), Nightboat Books (The United States) and *Poetry Aotearoa Yearbook.* They frequently work in sonic composition with artists and in film and theatre.

Francesca Leader is a writer, self-taught artist and former scholar from Montana. She writes fiction, poetry and essays and has been published both in Aotearoa New Zealand and overseas.

Freya Norris is a writer who lives in rural Kirikiriroa Hamilton. She is studying towards a master's in professional writing at the University of Waikato Te Whare Wānanga o Waikato, and has a partner, three children, one cat and 10 hens.

Geoff Sawers is a writer and artist whose fiction and criticism has been published in *Backwards Trajectory*, *Grey Sparrow Journal*, the *Times Literary Supplement* and *Unstamatic*.

Grace Lawrence is 18 and overwhelmed! She lives in Te Whanganui-a-Tara Wellington and in the hearts of people who enjoy sudoku.

Heidi North has won awards for both her poems and short stories, including an international Irish poetry prize, and she has been published in anthologies and magazines around the world. Heidi has a master's in creative writing from the Waipapa Taumata Rau University of Auckland; she was the New Zealand Fellow in the Shanghai International Writers Programme in 2016; and her first poetry collection, *Possibility of Flight*, was published in 2015 by Mākaro Press. Her second collection, *We are Tiny Beneath the Light* (The Cuba Press, 2019), was launched by U2, who used one of her poems on stage during their 2019 Joshua Tree Tour.

Holly H. Bercusson was born and raised with a love of letters in Tāmaki Makaurau Auckland. Add to that a complicated childhood, a personality disorder, a dash of Jewish neuroticism and you pretty much have a poet.

Iain Britton has published a number of collections in Aotearoa and the United Kingdom with Kilmog Press, Like This Press, Oystercatcher Press, Lapwing Publications, Interactive Press, Hesterglock Press and others. A new chapbook, *Project Constellation*, was published in the United Kingdom by Sampson Low in 2022.

Idoya Munn is an Ōtepoti-based queer writer and teacher who has previously published work in *Poetry Aotearoa Yearbook* and *Grief Almanac*.

Imé Corkery is a poet by choice and a chronic illness warrior by design. She has a master's in professional writing from the University of Waikato Te Whare Wānanga o Waikato. Her work looks at chronic illness advocacy through poetic storytelling, and her debut poetry collection *Persephone's Pancreas* is available on Amazon.

Iona Winter (Waitaha) is a kaituhi who lives in the Tasman region. Her multi-genre work can be found in numerous publications, spray-painted onto fences, and performed. She was the 2022 CLNZ/NZSA Writers' Award recipient and, fearless in the face of grief, she crafted *a liminal gathering: Elixir & Star Grief Almanac 2023*. Her toikupu *Intuit* sits atop the stunning FIFA World Cup mural around the Dunedin Town Hall. You can find Iona online or outside in the māra.

Jack Ross's most recent poetry collection is *The Oceanic Feeling* (Salt and Greyboy Press, 2021). He was the managing editor of *Poetry New Zealand Yearbook* (now

Poetry Aotearoa Yearbook) from 2014 to 2020, and has written and edited numerous other books, anthologies and literary journals. He lives with his wife, the crafter and art writer Bronwyn Lloyd, in Mairangi Bay Tāmaki Makaurau Auckland.

James Norcliffe has published 11 collections of poetry, including *Shadow Play* (Proverse, 2013), *Dark Days at the Oxygen Café* (Te Herenga Waka University Press, 2016), *Deadpan* (Otago University Press, 2019) and *Letter to 'Oumuamua* (Otago University Press, 2023). His recent work has appeared in *Landfall*, the *Cincinnati Review*, *Salamander*, *Gargoyle Magazine* and *Flash Fiction International*. In 2022 he was awarded the Prime Minister's Award for Literary Achievement in poetry.

Jan FitzGerald's work has appeared regularly in New Zealand literary journals since the 1970s and has been published overseas in the *Loch Raven Review*, the *Atlanta Review*, *Yellow Medicine Review*, *Meniscus*, *The London Magazine*, *Orbis*, *The High Window* and *Acumen*. She has published four poetry books, the latest of which is *A question bigger than a hawk* (The Cuba Press, 2022).

Jan Kemp MNZM is a New Zealand-born poet who lives in Kronberg im Taunus, Germany. Her most recent publications are her memoir *Raiment* (Massey University Press, 2022) and its sequel *To see a World* (Tranzlit, 2023). She hopes her tenth poetry collection, *dancing heart*, will appear in 2026, 50 years after the publication of her first book of poems, *Against the Softness of Woman* (Caveman Press, 1976).

Jan Napier is a Western Australian writer whose work has been showcased in anthologies and journals in Australia and overseas including in *Westerly 68.1* and the Canadian journal *Poetry Pacific*. Her villanelle 'Wiltshire 1840' won the Ethel Webb Blundell Poetry Prize in 2022.

Jane Matthews /ˈlɒɡə(ʊ)fʌɪl/ is a writer, reader, editor and tutor.

Jane Simpson, a Christchurch-based poet and historian, has two full-length collections, *A world without maps* (Interactive Press, 2016) and *Tuning Wordsworth's Piano* (Interactive Press, 2019). She won second prize in the New Zealand Poetry Society's 2023 International Poetry Competition. Her poems have most recently appeared in *Allegro Poetry Magazine*, *London Grip*, *Hamilton Stone Review*, *Otoliths*, *Poetry Aotearoa Yearbook* and *Catalyst*.

Janet Newman lives in Horowhenua. Her first poetry collection, *Unseasoned Campaigner* (Otago University Press, 2021), was the 2022 New Zealand Society of Authors Heritage Book Awards poetry winner. She completed her PhD at Massey University in 2019 with her thesis 'Imagining Ecologies: Traditions of Ecopoetry in Aotearoa New Zealand'.

Janet Wainscott lives near Ōtautahi Christchurch and writes poetry and essays. Her work has appeared in various literary magazines, including *takahē, Poetry Aotearoa Yearbook, Landfall* and *Catalyst*. Her first collection of poetry, *A Game of Swans*, was published by Sudden Valley Press in 2023.

Janis Freegard is the author of several poetry collections, most recently *Reading the Signs* (The Cuba Press, 2020), as well as a novel, *The Year of Falling* (Mākaro Press, 2015). Born in South Shields, England, she grew up in the United Kingdom, South Africa, Australia and Aotearoa, and has lived in Te Whanganui-a-Tara Wellington most of her life. She lives with an historian and works in the public service.

Jenny Powell is an Ōtepoti Dunedin writer and teacher. Her most recent collection is *Meeting Rita* (Cold Hub Press, 2021). She is the Dunedin City of Literature South D Poet Lorikeet.

Jessica Le Bas has published two collections of poetry: *Incognito* (2007) and *Walking to Africa* (2009), both with Auckland University Press. She won the Sarah Broom Prize for Poetry in 2019. Her 2010 children's novel *Staying Home: My True Diary of Survival* was re-released by Penguin Random House in 2021 as *Locked Down*. She lives in Waimea, Whakatū Nelson.

Jessica Thornley is a creative consultant, writer and mother who lives and works most of the time in Raglan Whāingaroa and some of the time in Rwanda. Alongside her work in social impact communications, Jess is studying towards a master's in professional writing at the University of Waikato Te Whare Wānanga o Waikato.

Jessie Burnette (she/they) is a PhD candidate and teaching fellow at the University of Waikato Te Whare Wānanga o Waikato. Her work has previously been published in *Mayhem* and *Poetry Aotearoa Yearbook*.

Joel LeBlanc is a queer writer, baker, chef and herbalist. His poetry has appeared in *Poetry Aotearoa Yearbook, Semaphore Magazine, takahē, Tarot* and more. He lives in Te Whanganui-a-Tara Wellington.

John Geraets lives in Whangārei and is curator of the online publications *remake* and *countertop*. His selected writings, *Everything's Something in Place*, was published by Titus Books in 2019.

John Tuke lives in Ōtautahi Christchurch and works as a gardener. His poem 'One of those days poetic' was written in homage to three North American poets, Tracy K. Smith, Ada Limón and Eileen Myles, as well as for his son, who lives in the United States. An earlier poem was published in the 2022 *Poetry New Zealand Yearbook*.

Keirryn Hintz is the proud mother of two girls and teaches in Kirikiriroa Hamilton. She dabbles in life drawing, writing and poetry, all usually half-finished and abandoned. She is especially interested in capturing the subtle drama and incidental humour of everyday life.

Keith Nunes is a writer whose poetry, fiction, haiku and visuals have been published around the globe. He creates ethereal manifestations as a way of communicating with the outside world.

Kerrin P. Sharpe has published five collections of poetry, the latest of which is *Hoof*, all with Te Herenga Waka University Press. Her poems have appeared in a wide range of journals including *Oxford Poets 13* (Carcanet Press), *Blackbox Manifold*, *Poetry*, *PN Review*, *berlin lit* and *Stand*.

Layal Moore teaches English and runs the writers' club at Mahurangi College, north of Auckland. Her poetry, short stories, artwork and photography have been published in *Poetry Aotearoa Yearbook*, *The Anthropozine*, *Mayhem* and *This Twilight Menagerie*. She lives in Wainui with her three children, four chickens and two guinea pigs.

Liam Hinton is a Kirikiriroa Hamilton-based poet. His work has been published in *Mayhem*, *Poetry Aotearoa Yearbook* and *Starling*. He co-runs One Question Theatre.

Liz Breslin is a writer, editor and performer of Polish and Irish descent, who lives in Ōtepoti Dunedin. Liz's poem collections are *In bed with the feminists* (Dead Bird Books, 2021; winner of the Kathleen Grattan Prize for a Sequence of Poems 2020), and *Alzheimer's and a spoon* (Otago University Press 2017), which was one of the *Listener*'s Top 100 books of 2017.

Loretta Riach is a writer who lives in Te Whanganui-a-Tara Wellington. They work with timescales and landscapes and are an avid collector of trinkets and fossils. Their poems have been published in *Sweet Mammalian*, *Starling*, *Minarets*, *Mayhem* and *takahē*. They are a facilitator at play_station artist-run space.

Lucy Miles is a teacher, journalist and writer who has a master's in English. She lives in Tāmaki Makaurau Auckland, and her poetry has been published in *Poetry Aotearoa Yearbook*.

Marcus Hobson is a writer and reviewer who has been published in *Mayhem*, the *Poetry Aotearoa Yearbook* and the *Listener*. He lives on the slopes of the Kaimai Range near Katikati, where he has enough space to hoard a vast collection of books.

Margaret Moores lives in Tāmaki Makaurau Auckland, where she and her husband own an indie bookshop. Her poems and flash fiction have been published in journals and anthologies in Aotearoa New Zealand and Australia.

Mark Prisco completed his PhD in English literature in 2023. His poetry has been published in *BlazeVOX*, *Mayhem*, *Poetry Aotearoa Yearbook* and *Minarets*. He was guest editor for *Mayhem* in 2021. He sometimes writes prose.

Medb Charleton is originally from Ireland. Her poetry has been published in *Landfall* and *Sport*, among other places. She is currently undertaking a PhD in English.

Megan Kitching lives in Ōtepoti Dunedin. Her poetry has appeared in many publications including the *Poetry Aotearoa Yearbook*, *takahē*, *Tarot* and *Landfall*. Her debut collection is *At the Point of Seeing* (Otago University Press, 2023).

Michael Giacon was born and raised in Tāmaki Makaurau Auckland in a Pākehā/ Italian family. He is on the board of the Samesame But Different LGBTQIA+ Writers Festival, for which he presents the annual Poetry Speakeasy and Open Mic in association with Auckland Libraries. His work has most recently appeared in editions of *a fine line*.

Michael Steven teaches electrical engineering, grows organic cannabis and occasionally writes poems. His most recent collection, *Night School*, was published in 2022 by Otago University Press.

Michelle Rahurahu is a writer heralding from Te Rotorua-nui-a-Kahumatamomoe and descends from Ngaati Raukawa, Ngaati Tahu-Ngaati Whaoa, Rangitaane and Contae Dhún na nGall. She currently resides on Ngaai Tuuaahuriri whenua.

Nathaniel Calhoun lives in the Far North of Aotearoa. He works with teams that monitor and restore biodiversity in ecosystems around the world. His poems are published widely, including in *New York Quarterly*, *Guesthouse*, *takahē*, *Azure*, *DMQ Review*, *Misfit Magazine*, *Quadrant*, *Hawaii Pacific Review* and *Landfall*.

Naveena Menon (she/her) is a queer writer who is working toward a master's in English at the University of Waikato Te Whare Wānanga o Waikato. Her words have previously appeared in *Sweet Mammalian* and *Overcom*.

Nicholas Wright is a lecturer in the English department at the University of Canterbury Te Whare Wānanga o Waitaha. He is currently working on a book of essays on contemporary poetry in Aotearoa.

Nicola Andrews (Māori, Pākehā) is a member of the Ngāti Paoa iwi and lives on Ramaytush Ohlone territory. Last year they won the 2023 AAALS Indigenous Writers Prize for Poetry, and published two chapbooks: *Sentimental Value* (Ghost City Press) and *Māori Maid Difficult* (Tram Editions). They work as a librarian.

Nigel Skjellerup works in the Ōtautahi Christchurch healthcare community as an anaesthetist. His poems have been published in the *Press, takahē, Mayhem, Catalyst, New Zealand Poetry Society Anthology* and *Poetry Aotearoa Yearbook*.

Olivia Macassey is a poet and editor whose poems have previously appeared in the *Poetry Aotearoa Yearbook, takahē, Otoliths, Landfall, Rabbit* and other places. She is the author of two books of poetry.

Owen Bullock's latest poetry collection is *Pancakes for Neptune* (Recent Work Press, 2023). He has also published three other poetry titles, five books of haiku, a bilingual edition of tanka, and a novella. He works in the creative writing and literary studies department at the University of Canberra.

Paula Harris (1973–2023) lived in Palmerston North. She won the 2018 Janet B. McCabe Poetry Prize and the 2017 Lilian Ida Smith Award. Her writing has been published in various journals, including *The Sun, Pleiades, Passages North, New Delta Review, Prelude* and *Aotearotica*.

Penelope Scarborough studies psychology and philosophy, around which most of her writing revolves, at Te Herenga Waka Victoria University of Wellington. She was a finalist for the National Schools Poetry Award in 2021.

Philip Armstrong teaches writing and literary studies at the University of Canterbury Te Whare Wānanga o Waitaha. His poetry collection, *Sinking Lessons*, was published by Otago University Press in 2020.

Rachael Elliott's work has been published in places such as *JAAM, Mayhem* and the *Poetry Aotearoa Yearbook*. Excerpts of her work-in-progress were shortlisted for the Sargeson Prize in 2019. She has a master's in creative writing from the University of Waikato Te Whare Wānanga o Waikato and lives in Rotongaro.

Riemke Ensing was born in The Netherlands, in 1939. She immigrated to New Zealand with her parents at the age of 12 in 1951 and grew up in Dargaville. At this stage of her life she spoke no English. In 1967 she was appointed as a tutor in the Department of English at the University of Auckland, where she taught until 1999. Her poetry is represented extensively in anthologies, and her most recent publications are *If Only* (Pear Tree Press, 2017) and *Watermarks* (Janus Press, 2019) with prints by Claire van Vliet.

Sara Al-Bahar is a third-year English student from the Waikato. Her work has previously been published in *Mayhem* and printed in local zines. She clutches onto the dream of a peaceful world and a quiet home overlooking a large body of water.

Sarah-Kate Simons is a writer and poet who is originally from rural Canterbury and now lives in Tauranga. She is widely published in journals and anthologies. She has been shortlisted and placed in many writing competitions locally and internationally, and was a judge for the 2022 New Zealand Poetry Society haiku junior competition. Her hobbies include ballet, art and verbal sparring matches with her characters.

Shaun Stockley lives in Manawatū and has been published in *Young Writers* in the United Kingdom and in the *Poetry Aotearoa Yearbook*.

Shivani Agrawal is a poet and editor from India who has a long-standing love affair with Aotearoa. She is pursuing a master's in professional writing at the University of Waikato Te Whare Wānanga o Waikato. Recent work has appeared in *Mayhem, Mister Magazine, The Alipore Post* and *The Uncuts*. She is the co-founder of Femme Fridays, a virtual workshop for South Asian women and queer writers.

Sophia Wilson grew up on unceded Anaiwan land in Australia and is now based in rural Ōtepoti Dunedin. An arts graduate, mother of three and former mental health worker, she is the author of *Sea Skins*, a poetry collection published by Flying Island Books in 2023.

Sophie Rae-Jordan likes the way poetry can make her feel both big and small at the same time. Her work can be found in *Mayhem, Symposia, Sweet Mammalian, Moist Poetry Journal, Poetry Aotearoa Yearbook* and more.

Stu Bagby is an editor and poet who was born in Te Kōporu and now lives in Pāremoremo. His work appeared in *AUP New Poets 2*, and his first collection, *As It Was in the Beginning* (Steele Roberts, 2005), was nominated by the *Sunday Star-Times* as one of the best books of that year. He has written four books of poetry and a play, and has edited three anthologies. In 2000 he won the New Zealand Poetry Society's International Poetry Competition.

Tunmise Adebowale is a year 13 student at St Hilda's Collegiate School in Ōtepoti Dunedin. Her poem 'A Little Grace' won first prize in the 2023 *Poetry Aotearoa Yearbook* student poetry competition. She is a Nigerian-born New Zealand writer and writes from her experience as a third-culture kid: born in Nigeria, raised in South Africa and living in New Zealand. Her work has been published on NZ Poetry Shelf, Verb Wellington, *Re-Draft* and Canadian theatre company Theatrefolk's *BIPOC Voices and Perspectives Monologue* 2021 collection.

Vaughan Rapatahana (Te Āti Awa) commutes between homes in Hong Kong SAR, the Philippines and Aotearoa New Zealand. He is widely published across several genres in both of his main languages, te reo Māori and English, and his work has been translated into Bahasa Malaysia, Italian, French, Mandarin, Romanian and Spanish. He is the author and editor or co-editor of over 40 books.

Victor Billot is an Ōtepoti Dunedin writer. His poetry collection *The Sets* was published by Otago University Press in 2021.

Wes Lee lives in Te Whanganui-a-Tara Wellington. She has three poetry collections. Her work has appeared in an array of publications, including *Ōrangahau | Best New Zealand Poems*, *Westerly*, *The London Magazine*, *Landfall*, *The Stinging Fly* and *Cordite Poetry Review*. Most recently she was awarded the Heroines/Joyce Parkes Women's Writing Prize 2022 in New South Wales and shortlisted for the *Poetry London* Pamphlet Prize 2023 in the United Kingdom.

Willow Noir lives with her sister in south Taranaki, where she figures out the convolutions of her mind through poetry, collage and the rhythm of her crochet hooks. Her work has been published in *Tarot*.

Wren Boyer is a gender-queer teacher, writer and poet who lives in the Waikato. Their writing explores themes of gender, parenthood, relationships and trauma, and they write everything from poetry and micro-fiction to longer form prose and plays. They have performed and published in the Short+Sweet festival, *Mayhem*, *The Siren's Call*, *Beyond Words*, To Hull & Back, *WritersWeekly* and *72 Hours of Insanity*.

Poetry Aotearoa Yearbook, founded by Louis Johnson in 1951 as the *Poetry New Zealand Yearbook*, is New Zealand's longest-running poetry magazine. It has been edited by some of New Zealand's most distinguished poets and academics, including Elizabeth Caffin, Grant Duncan, Riemke Ensing, Bernard Gadd, Leonard Lambert, Harry Ricketts, Elizabeth Smither, Brian Turner, Alistair Paterson, Jack Ross and Johanna Emeney. It is now edited by Dr Tracey Slaughter of the University of Waikato Te Whare Wānanga o Waikato. The university's financial support of the *Yearbook* is much appreciated.

Managing editor
Tracey Slaughter
editor@poetrynz.net
Website: www.poetrynz.net

Submissions: The submission dates for each issue are between 1 May and 31 July of each year. Email submissions are preferred. Email submissions and a covering letter should go to editor@poetrynz.net. Please paste your poems in the body of the message or include them as a single MS Word file attachment.

Submissions by post and a covering letter should be sent to: Dr Tracey Slaughter, English Programme, School of Arts, University of Waikato, Private Bag 3105, Hamilton 3240. Posted submissions will not be returned.

Please include a short biographical note and your current postal address with your submission. Contributors whose poems are selected will receive a free copy of the issue in which their work is included.

First published in 2024 by Massey University Press
Private Bag 102904, North Shore Mail Centre
Auckland 0745, New Zealand
www.masseypress.ac.nz

Cover design by Jo Bailey
Typesetting by Megan van Staden

Extracts and images published with permission:
page 187: 'The Dry Salvages', by T. S. Eliot, courtesy of Faber & Faber;
page 225: *UNPACKING the BODY*, by Joanna Margaret Paul, courtesy of
Magdalena Harris and Christchurch Art Gallery Te Puna o Waiwhetū.

A catalogue record for this book is available from the National Library of
New Zealand

Printed and bound in China by Everbest Printing Investment Limited

ISBN: 978-1-99-101670-6

The assistance of Creative New Zealand is gratefully acknowledged by
the publisher

Poetry Aotearoa Yearbook 2024 is published in association
with the University of Waikato Te Whare Wānanga o Waikato